Spiritual
Greatness—
Studies
in
Exodus

Spiritual
Greatness –
Studies in Exodus

Tom Julien

BMH Books
Winona Lake, Indiana 46590

"These studies are dedicated to my faithful co-workers in Brethren Missions in Europe.

May they know spiritual greatness in their high calling."

Cover photo by Charles W. Turner

ISBN: 0-88469-121-7

COPYRIGHT 1979
BMH BOOKS
WINONA LAKE, INDIANA

Printed in U.S.A.

Introduction

These studies from the Book of Exodus are mainly concerned with the man Moses, and are an attempt to discover some of the reasons for his spiritual greatness.

Moses was unique in history. After being saved from death through the intervention of an Egyptian princess, he spent the first 40 years of his life in the court of Pharoah. His consciousness of a divine destiny ripened, and, in an extraordinary manifestation of faith, he identified himself with his suffering brethren, the enslaved Israelites. Faith was quickly followed by folly, expressed in the impetuous murder of an Egyptian taskmaster, that sent Moses to the desert for the second period of 40 years. In the desert God made him into the man He could use.

From a burning bush God called Moses back to Egypt, to be the central figure of one of the strangest dramas ever enacted. A series of miraculous interventions brought Egypt, with its Pharoah, to its knees. The visit of the death angel and the passage of the Red Sea tore the Israelites from their captivity and landed them, emotionally and physically drained, in the desert where Moses began his third and most difficult period of 40 years.

Moses received the law of God on Mount Sinai. Yet, at the

very time God was meeting this great man on the summit, the Children if Israel fell into debauchery. In fury Moses shattered the tables of the law, ground the golden calf into powder, scattered it upon the water and forced the sinning people to drink it. This was the hour of Moses' greatest crisis, the hour when his greatness reached its pinnacle. And it was then that God gave one of His greatest promises, "My presence shall go with thee, and I will give thee rest."

By the time you reach the end of these studies, you will know Moses much better. But this is not the principal reason for the studies; it is that through Moses we might know God better, and through this knowledge learn to better know ourselves. Throughout this book God's concern is that men might know that He is the Lord. When we really know that He is the Lord of the events of our lives, we begin to know something of the spiritual greatness that we find in the life of Moses.

Yes, Moses was unique in history. But in a special way, so is each of us. We shall never live the extraordinary miracles Moses experienced in Egypt, but within each of us is the potential for greatness. The important thing in our study of Moses is not the events in his life, but the way he responded to those events. Whether or not we become great men and women for God depends not on the circumstances of life, but the way we respond to those circumstances.

There are many books written to tell us how to live the Christian life, and some of them are quite helpful. But spiritual greatness does not come through reading books. It comes through knowing God intimately in the crises and desert experiences of our lives, discovering in Him our destiny, and allowing Him to be the Lord of our lives.

It would certainly be a pity for you to study through Exodus hurriedly, or in a detached way. Take time to allow yourself to be gripped by the momentous events it portrays. Learn to share Moses' emotion in his times of crisis. Allow God's Spirit to cause these pages to come alive, so that their study will be a transforming experience in your life.

Table of Contents

	Introduction	5
1.	Times and Destiny	9
2.	Moses' Colossal Blunder	19
3.	A Divine Commission	29
4.	The Return to Egypt	41
5.	God's Mighty Hand	53
6.	Judgment and Deliverance	65
7.	Salvation of the Lord	77
8.	Mountains and Valleys	87
9.	Desert Provisions	97
10.	Harassments	109
11.	The Will of Jehovah	121
12.	A Rebellious People	131
13.	Jehovah of Glory	143

I

Times and Destiny

Exodus 1:7—2:10

I. Times (Exod. 1:7-22)
   1. Israel in glory (v. 7)
   2. Israel in bondage (vv. 8-22)
   3. Israel's spiritual deterioration
   4. God's people today

II. Destiny (Exod. 2:1-10)
   1. Divine intervention (vv. 5-6)
   2. Human faith (vv. 1-4)
   3. Moses' preparation (vv. 7-10)
   4. Modern men of destiny

Never have we lived in more critical times. Ours is a day when all the old values are under attack and the spirit of relativism has permeated nearly every sphere of life. The average man finds himself adrift in a river of confusion with none of the familiar landmarks to guide him.

Nowhere is this confusion more evident than in religion. The religion page of Sunday's newspaper reads like an ecclesiastical fairy tale. Confusion reigns in the liberal circles. But those of us who know the truth are too often characterized by pettiness. In a world crying for spiritual greatness, why do we so often find among God's people a shabbiness of character sometimes unequaled by those who do not pretend to be Christians? Few seem preoccupied with the glory of Christ, and their witness is neutralized by the sheer weight of multiplied little things.

We begin the study of the Exodus accounts of one of the greatest men the world has known—Moses. He was unique in history; none of us will ever be like him. Yet, we can discover from these verses of Scripture some of the reasons for his greatness.

The need is great for Christians who will live extraordinary lives for God.

Though greatness defies definition, all great men have been characterized by a sensitivity to two things: their times and their destiny.

They have the ability to identify themselves with their times and their people. They are sensitive to the significance of trends that pass unnoticed by the masses. They are deeply moved by the suffering of their brothers.

But great men do what lesser men cannot do: they rise above circumstances, for they are conscious of their destiny. They are willing to fight the current—to dominate instead of being dominated. This accounts for their singleness of purpose. Long after the fire of emotions has subsided, and usually against senseless criticism, they forge ahead.

Well over 3,000 years ago, in the land of Egypt, God's

people were being severely tried. The times were ripe for the appearance of a man of uncommon destiny. This is the story of how God provided such a man.

I. Times (Exod. 1:7-22)

When the story of the Book of Exodus begins, the Children of Israel are in the land of Egypt. How they came to be there is one of the fascinating stories of the Bible. Joseph, sold into slavery by his jealous brothers, entered Egypt in humiliation. But though the brothers had purposed Joseph's harm, God used their wickedness for His glory, and exalted Joseph to a position second only to the king. Ruling over the land, he brought his father Jacob and all his brothers into Egypt in glory and established them in the best part of the land.

1. Israel in glory (v. 7). When Jacob parted for Egypt to see his long-lost son, God appeared to him at night in a vision saying, "Fear not to go down into Egypt, for I will there make of thee a great nation." The Pharaoh who had befriended Joseph was probably of the Hyksos dynasty. These were distant cousins of the Israelites, and were doubtless favorable to their development as a nation. This, plus the fact that Egypt was a healthful country, favored the rapid development of the nation until the "land was filled with them."

The sojourn in Egypt therefore was used by God to form this people into a great nation. Years before when God had appeared to Abram, He had said, "I will make of thee a great nation, and I will bless thee, and make thy name great; and thou shalt be a blessing; and I will bless them that bless thee and curse him that curseth thee: and in thee shall all the families of the earth be blessed" (Gen. 12:2-3).

From impossible beginnings—an aged man and his barren wife—God had formed a mighty people, and the first part of His promise to Abram was now fulfilled.

2. Israel in bondage (vv. 8-22). Yet, a mark of Israel's spiritual heritage was that she should remain distinct from the other nations of the world. It was only in this way that she could remain pure, and thus be a blessing to all the nations of the world. To ensure Israel's separation, God promised Abram the land of Canaan.

We do not know why the Children of Israel continued to live in Egypt after the death of Joseph. But the fact is that they did remain, planting their roots more and more deeply in this land that was to remain foreign to them. They gradually forgot God's promise to Abram, plus their spiritual heritage and mission.

Then tragedy struck. The Hyksos dynasty fell, and these kings who were friendly to the Jews were driven from the land. Israel's favored position was lost; the enmity of the Egyptians was turned against all who were associated with the former kings. Through the years that followed, the condition of the Hebrews steadily declined.

Gradually the Israelites were looked upon as a threat to the Egyptians. The existence of such a large and powerful foreign bloc within their boundaries caused the Egyptians to fear lest the Israelites should turn against them in time of invasion. Drastic measures were taken.

Thus the Children of Israel fell from their glory to become slaves to the Egyptians, just as Joseph had been when he first entered the country. The king set taskmasters over them and made them build his royal cities, hoping to weaken them, but the more they were afflicted, the more they grew.

Seeing that this did not diminish their power, Pharaoh ordered the two chief midwives to have all male children killed upon birth. And when this too failed, he sent out a royal decree that all sons born to the Israelites should be cast into the Nile.

God's chosen people were threatened with extinction in a foreign land.

3. **Israel's spiritual deterioration.** It is risky to teach from silence, but between verses 7 and 8 something must have happened to the nation Israel. It is impossible to believe that

any king in Egypt could so easily make slaves out of the powerful Israelites unless we assume that God's people, as well as the land of Egypt, must have undergone a change.

Around 300 years elapsed between the death of Joseph and the birth of Moses, and we can only conclude that these were years of spiritual deterioration for Israel. Not that they had adopted the religion of Egypt—there is no evidence of this—but simply that they had fallen deeply in love with this land of leeks and garlic, of melons and cucumbers. Even though they retained their national identity, they had become too comfortable in a place where they did not permanently belong.

If we read that the Egyptians were able to enslave a people "more and mightier" than they, it can only be because this people had lost its spiritual vitality. There had been a gradual corrosion of the old values inherited from Abraham, and an imperceptible accommodation to the ways of the Egyptians.

And seemingly there was no one who could discern the times and turn back the trend. By the time tragedy struck, it was too late.

4. God's people today. Paul, writing to the Christians of Corinth, said that the things which happened to the Israelites were to be examples for us, and that they are written for our admonition (1 Cor. 10:11).

In saying this we do not mean that the nation Israel of the Old Testament is the same thing as the church of the New Testament. To make one a type of the other leads to unwarranted comparisons.

Nevertheless, the Christian, like the nation Israel, has a special calling. We are called out of the world to become the people of God. We are given the blessing of God so that through us the nations of the earth might be blessed.

Like Israel in Egypt, we find ourselves sojourners in a foreign land. Our citizenship is in heaven, but we are on the earth. Though we are in the world, we are not, and must never be, of the world. We are in contact with the world daily—we work in its shops and offices; we participate in its activities. But we realize that its values must not become our values, that its goals are not the same as our goals.

There is always the danger that the Christian will become a slave to this world, just as Israel did in Egypt. But this slavery is not a sudden thing. It does not involve the denial of our religion, or falling into deep sin. It is simply the result of a gradual corrosion of spiritual values, of an imperceptible accommodation to the world in which we live. Instead of giving ourselves to God and His glory, we give ourselves to the leeks and garlic of the strange land we inhabit.

And often by the time we awaken to our condition, we find ourselves already in abject slavery.

It is my sad conviction that vast areas of the evangelical church are enslaved to this world without even being aware of it. We pride ourselves for not smoking and drinking, for abstaining from movies and dancing, and for not playing cards, seemingly unaware that the world is something different and far more subtle.

In fact, for too many Christians separation from the world merely means avoiding unsaved people and the places they go. We have created a "Christian" counterpart for nearly all the worldly taboos, and our conscience remains untroubled as long as we find our amusements with professing Christians.

But are we willing to take a hard look at the values we have established? Is there really any essential difference between our lives and the lives of our unsaved neighbors, except for the fact that we conform to our church pattern and build our social life around other church people? Are our decisions prompted by an inner spiritual force, or have we allowed ourselves to be squeezed into the mold of our generation?

If some of us could compare what we are today with what we were 20 years ago, we would be appalled by the degree of spiritual deterioration that has occurred. But spread over a period of 20 years, the day-by-day corrosion has passed unnoticed.

The cure for worldliness is not to erect a new set of taboos. It is first of all to be able to discern the times—to see that we are living in evil days and that some of us have fallen hopelessly in love with the world.

When we have done this, the next step is to rediscover our spiritual destiny.

II. Destiny (Exod. 2:1-10)

We turn now to the verses narrating the birth of the man God would use to bring deliverance to His people—Moses.

In reading this account, we should attempt to feel something of the tragedy surrounding the birth of a male child in Egypt at this time. It is possible for us to read the biblical stories coldly—to forget that the parents of Moses were of the same flesh and blood as we. The news of the birth of a son is something that under normal conditions brings great joy. But for Amram and Jochebed (Exod. 6:20) it struck terror, for Pharaoh had decreed the death of all males born to the Israelites.

Moses' mother saw that he was a "goodly child." Perhaps even then she caught a glimpse of God's destiny for her son. After having hid him for three months at home, she decided on a drastic move. Knowing that the king's daughter was accustomed to bathing at a certain spot in the Nile, she constructed a small ark out of the bulrushes and hid the child among the river flags.

And it worked! The Egyptian princess was filled with compassion at the sight of the Hebrew babe and saved him from death.

1. Divine intervention (vv. 5-6). One cannot read this story without seeing the divine imprint upon it. In fact, those who do not believe in a personal God who can intervene in the affairs of man are forced to call this account, and others like it, mere legends of Hebrew antiquity.

Yet, the account is too ingenious to be legend: only God could step into the hopeless tragedy of the Israelites and use the very methods meant for their destruction to provide their deliverance. Had Pharaoh not decreed such drastic measures against the Jews, Moses would have grown up like every other Hebrew lad. But because of the death decree, Moses was taken into the king's court and given the preparation essential for his future mission of delivering his people. Do not miss the divine irony: the very ones who were seeking to destroy God's people were used by God to prepare the future deliverer.

In reading these verses we do well to remember that from God's viewpoint situations are never hopeless. For God is able to use the wrath of men to praise Him.

2. Human faith (vv. 1-4). God's deliverance is never independent of man's faith. God led Pharaoh's daughter to the crying baby and filled her heart with compassion, but only because the parents of Moses, acting on faith alone, were willing to construct the ark. Hebrews 11:23 says, "By faith Moses, when he was born, was hid three months of his parents, because they saw he was a proper child; they were not afraid of the king's commandment."

Faith, according to Phillips' translation of Hebrews 11:1, means "putting our full confidence in the things we hope for; it means being certain of things we cannot see." Faith is characterized by a complete confidence in God's power, and by a certainty that God will act. Faith is the link which joins man to God, allowing His supernatural power to manifest itself.

Now, faith in the biblical sense means more than simply believing something intellectually—it means acting on the basis of our believing. The parents of Moses manifested their faith in God not simply by forcing themselves to believe God would save their son, but by actually constructing the ark and putting their child in the river. No doubt they did so with fear and trembling—and possibly severe doubts. But they acted, and it is in real-life situations such as this that faith operates.

God can work in impossible situations, but ours must be

more than a theoretical faith. There is a tendency among too many Christians to accept our Christianity without personal involvement. We want to experience Christian love, but we do not care to love our brethren. We want to be men of faith, but we seem unwilling to manifest this faith in difficult life situations.

3. Moses' preparation (vv. 7-10). It is in these verses that the genius of God's plan is seen. While the baby Moses lay floating among the flags of the river, his sister Miriam hid in the reeds to await the outcome. Immediately upon the discovery of the child, she was on the scene, offering to find a "nurse of the Hebrew women." Thus Moses was carried back in safety to his own mother, who for the first three years (according to Josephus) of his life had the full responsibility of his training and was even paid for it! Then, at the age of three, the child became the adopted son of the Egyptian princess. In the years following, Moses received the training of an Egyptian prince.

Moses was therefore a man who learned two cultures. Later in life he would be equally at ease with the people of God and the people of Egypt. It was only because of his unique training that Moses was able to fulfill his spiritual destiny.

4. Modern men of destiny. Just as Moses was saved from destruction and destined to a great spiritual ministry, so are we who call ourselves Christians. The times are equally significant. Where are our modern men of destiny who will be able to be witnesses of genuine Christianity in this day of confusion?

To fulfill his mission Moses had to stand between two worlds and know them both: the world of the Israelites and the world of the Egyptians. Modern men of destiny, too, stand between two kingdoms: the kingdom of God and the kingdom of Satan. To be effective witnesses, they must know something of both, and be able to move with ease among both men of God and men of the world.

For too long we have confused separation from the world

with isolation from the world. But Jesus never taught isolation. The evangelical church finds itself increasingly out of contact with the people to whom she must witness. The content of our message must never change, but it must be made relevant to the people of our generation. We must be willing to sit where they sit and to be sensitive to the problems of their existence. The Gospel must be applied to their lives, not just the lives of their grandparents.

We do not know at what period of life Moses fully realized his divine destiny. Stephen, in his address before the Sanhedrin, implies that by the time he was 40 he "understood that God by his hand would deliver his brethren." Perhaps it was when he began to ponder the intriguing story of his childhood deliverance that he realized he was chosen of God for a special task. But whenever it might have been, imagine the thrill that he experienced.

Perhaps some reading these words will experience the same thrill, realizing that they, too, are men of destiny.

Questions for Discussion

1. What are some marks of spiritual greatness?
2. What are some marks of spiritual pettiness?
3. Are the times in which we live essentially different from those of our forefathers?
4. How can I tell whether I am in bondage to the world?
5. Does God intervene in history today? Examples.
6. What are the characteristics of a faith life?
7. Is our presentation of the Gospel to twentieth-century man effective?

2

Moses' Colossal Blunder

Exodus 2:11-25

▲▲▲▲▲▲▲▲▲▲▲▲▲▲▲▲▲▲▲▲▲▲▲▲▲▲▲▲▲

I. Human Impotence (Exod. 2:11-15)
   1. Moses' consciousness of his destiny (Acts 7:23-25)
   2. Moses' visit to his brethren (v. 11)
   3. Moses' act of faith (Heb. 11:24-26)
   4. Moses' tragic blunder (vv. 12-15)

II. The Desert Experience (Exod. 2:15-22)
   1. God's provision (vv. 16-22)
   2. The meaning of the desert experience

III. Divine Readiness (Exod. 2:23-25)
   1. Egypt was ready (v. 23)
   2. God was ready (vv. 24-25)

Paul, speaking of the thorn in the flesh used by Satan to buffet him, exclaimed, "When I am weak, then I am strong."

In uttering these words Paul stated a great spiritual truth, the same truth with which Jesus began His beatitudes, saying, "Blessed are the poor in spirit," or as another translator has put it, "Blessed are those who realize their spiritual poverty."

Spiritual greatness is a quality which is directly related to humility. By humility we do not mean a pious self-abasement; truly humble people realize that they are created in God's image, and are therefore beings of great value. Real humility is the ability to see ourselves in relation to God, and to realize that apart from God we have no spiritual resources—that our sufficiency is of Christ.

Every great man of God has had to learn this lesson. Some learn it easily; others learn only at the expense of great personal suffering. Such a man was Moses, who was required to spend 40 years of his life in the desert in order to learn that God's work must be done in God's way.

The first 40 years of Moses' life are passed over virtually in silence by the Scriptures. Stephen, speaking before the Sanhedrin, states that Moses "was instructed in all the wisdom of the Egyptians; and he was mighty in his words and works" (Acts 7:22). The Jewish historian Josephus tells us that Moses became an illustrious soldier, and that he led the Egyptian troops against the Ethiopian city of Moroe, which he took.

Whether or not Josephus' account is true, Moses' human qualifications for the task to which God was calling him were superb. Jewish in birth, he manifested all the genius of the Hebrew temperament. His training was the finest that Egypt could offer, and Egyptian civilization was nearing its highest point at this time. It is said that the great university of Heliopolis, on the banks of the Nile, drew from all parts of the civilized world up to 10,000 students.

But the story of this chapter is that human excellence is never sufficient in itself to do God's work. And to substitute human zeal for divine power is to set the stage for tragedy.

I. Human Impotence (Exod. 2:11-15)

1. Moses' consciousness of his destiny (Acts 7:23-25). From his mother's knee, Moses had learned of the great Jehovah, the creator of heaven and earth. He had doubtless heard how God had called his ancestor Abraham into the land of promise and given him assurance of national blessing.

As he grew up in the Egyptian palaces, he could never forget his Jewish birth and the unusual circumstances of his early childhood. Then one day Moses came to the consciousness that "God by his hand would deliver his brethren." Perhaps this came through a direct revelation from God. Most likely, however, it was simply a growing conviction, fed by the affliction of his suffering brethren.

The consciousness of his divine calling must have had an electrifying effect on Moses. Never again would he be the same. Most of us Christians can still remember the excitement we felt when we realized for the first time that we had been chosen by God for a specific purpose—that God had a will for our lives. It is God's call that lifts our lives out of the vanity of day-by-day existence and gives them meaning. And when men find meaning in life, there is nothing they refuse to do.

2. Moses' visit to his brethren (v. 11). Moses was now grown: Stephen tells us in Acts that he was 40 years old. His Egyptian training was finished; Jewish history says he had been engaged in Egyptian military service. But in the hours of his greatest success, he did not forget his brethren.

This visit to his brethren changed the course of his life. He had doubtless been aware of the terrible conditions of the Jewish slaves at work on the Egyptian monuments, but now he was seeing firsthand their suffering. His heart was filled with compassion.

3. Moses' act of faith (Heb. 11:24-26). The writer of Hebrews gives us a magnificent account of what happened on that visit to the oppressed Hebrew slaves. For it was doubtless on this occasion that Moses exercised his great act of faith and formally decided to identify himself with his kinsmen. He chose to suffer affliction with the people of God, rather than to enjoy the pleasures of sin for a season. He esteemed the reproach of Christ greater riches than the treasures of Egypt.

Sitting in the comfort of our living room, we find it difficult to apprehend the implications of Moses' decision on that memorable day. In the history of the world, few, if any, have made so complete and drastic a human sacrifice for the cause of God. The mighty pyramids of Egypt, though tremendously impressive, cannot convey to the modern traveler the earthly glory of ancient Egypt at the summit of her greatness, and Moses shared all this glory. Nor can we in the twentieth century grasp the magnitude of human suffering represented by the slaves at whose cost the Egyptian pharaohs had constructed their glory. To exchange the one for the other was humanly unthinkable. But Moses' sights were set beyond the passing glory of Egypt, and he knew God's hand to be upon him. And in faith, he made his decision.

4. **Moses' tragic blunder (vv. 12-15).** What a study in contrasts! From his noble act of faith in which he chooses to identify himself with his people, Moses plunges to an act of human folly. Among other heart-rending scenes in the slave camp was that of an Egyptian smiting a Hebrew who was unable to fulfill the fierce demands of the taskmaster. Moses looked "this way and that way," and seeing they were alone, he impetuously slew the Egyptian and hid him in the sand.

The consequences of this deed followed quickly. The following day Moses attempted to separate two Hebrews who were striving together. One immediately spat out, "Who made you a prince and a judge over us? Do you intend to kill me just as you killed the Egyptian yesterday?" Thus the Hebrew slave that Moses had wished to befriend had talked, and the news of the slaying was out.

Soon after, the king was informed. Moses' Jewish birth certainly raised rumors of insurrection, and Pharaoh decreed drastic measures: a man of the stature of Moses befriending the Hebrews could not be tolerated; he must be put to death.

Through one rash, violent act Moses lost not only his favored place with the Egyptians, but worse still, he seemingly lost all chance of fulfilling his divine mission. To save his life he fled to the Sinai desert.

Let us attempt to learn the lesson of Moses' impetuous deed. On the one hand, there was nothing at all wrong with the faith of Moses when he decided to commit his life to God. This faith is commended in the New Testament.

Moses' error was that this faith did not extend to the methods he chose to deliver his people. He was not willing to wait on God. The great Moses felt that he was sufficient in himself to do God's work.

Examples such as this abound in the Scriptures. Think of Abraham and the promise God gave him that he would be the father of a great nation. Humanly speaking, this was impossible, for his wife was barren; but Abraham was willing to believe that with God all things are possible. Yet in the months that followed, Abraham and Sarah began to get fidgety. Surely God could not have meant that Sarah herself would be the mother of Abraham's son, they reasoned. Surely God did not expect them just to await the impossible; they must get busy and help God keep His promise. So it was that Abraham yielded to the carnal reasoning of Sarah, and took her servant as his wife. But this was not what God meant when he promised a miracle, and with every Arab-Jewish war today the Jews still pay a price for Abraham's refusal to wait on God, for the Arabs are the descendants of Abraham's carnal act.

Moses' blunder is typical of one of the most serious faults among Christians today. We commit our lives to God, and this commitment is often genuine. But from then on, God is often left on the shelf. Much of our Christian education operates on the philosophy that once we become "great in word and in deed," we shall be able to really get things done for God. Much of so-called Christian service is simply human ingenuity. Because something gets results in the world, we figure that it ought to get the same kind of results in the church. With the world's methods we attempt to do the work of God; then we have the audacity to ask God to bless our carnal efforts.

Jesus said on one occasion, "That which is born of the flesh is flesh." To be sure, He was not talking about church programs, but the truth He stated can apply to the whole field of Christian work. No amount of praying is going to change our carnal projects into something spiritual. God's work must be done in God's way.

The New Testament reveals plainly that Christian service is not man working for God, but rather God working through man. My only hope of spiritual glory is Christ in me; only as I give Him the liberty to use my body for His purposes can I know a measure of spiritual greatness.

This does not mean that God ignores our talents and our training. All that we possess and all that we can secure make us more valuable in His service. But all must be laid at His feet. To shove aside the Spirit is to quench Him. And it is in such moments of self-sufficiency that blunders are made, such as changed the course of Moses' life.

II. The Desert Experience (Exod. 2:15-22)

In the latter part of verse 15 one can almost sense some of the gnawing frustration that Moses must have felt after his flight from Pharaoh. For 40 years he had known the comforts and the glory of the greatest civilization known to the world. He had been accustomed to king's palaces and had experienced the taste of power and victory. He had come into the consciousness of a great divine mission and by a supreme act of faith had thrown himself on the side of his brethren. But one act of folly had ruined all, and now he was a hunted fugitive in the burning desert. As he sat by the well to refresh himself, he must have felt utter despair.

1. God's provision (vv. 16-22). But God had not forgotten Moses. The king of Egypt had a treaty with the neighboring Hittite king to the effect that fugitives along the northern route to Syria should be arrested and sent back. This was doubtless known to Moses, and for this reason he fled to the Sinai peninsula, inhabited by the Midianites. The Midianites were a group of tribes descended from Abraham and Keturah (Gen. 25:1-4). It is possible that they still retained worship of the true Jehovah. Reuel, later called Jethro, was a priest and his name means "a friend of God."

Moses, still the helper of the oppressed, aided the seven daughters of Reuel by allowing them to water their father's flock. Befriended, he decided to remain with Reuel's family and was married to Zipporah, one of the daughters.

Thus Moses was given a home and protection during his stay in the wilderness. But how different from the palaces of Egypt! And the depression that Moses must have felt is reflected in the name he gave his firstborn son, Gershom, which means "a stranger here."

2. The meaning of the desert experience. God is a God of mercy and grace; His grace extends even to His impetuous children who so often forget Him in their haste. "Like as a father pitieth his children, so the Lord pitieth them that fear him. For he knoweth our frame; he remembereth that we are dust" (Psa. 103:13-14). God was not through with Moses.

In fact, God's grace is such that He can even make use of our acts of folly to bring His plan to perfection, for the desert years were a part of God's will for His servant. Moses had received the finest training the world could give him. Now in the solitude of the wilderness God would be his teacher. The lessons he would learn during those 40 long years of loneliness could never be learned in the classrooms of Egypt's universities.

Nearly all of God's servants have had their desert experiences. Certainly none of them chose willingly to leave the limelight or to be torn from the things or places they loved, and for many this experience has been the result of an act of folly similar to that of Moses. Some, rather than seek God's face and learn His lessons, have rebelled and thus proved their unfitness for a future ministry. But those who have responded to God's Spirit during these times of forced absence from the heat of the battle will admit that solitude has been a necessary step in their spiritual development.

The desert taught Moses humility. The Moses who left Egypt was a man who was great in word and in deed, but he was not yet great in the sight of God. The proud Moses had to be broken. Moses had led victorious armies. Now he must learn to pasture sheep. As an Egyptian prince he had learned to give orders. Now he must learn to accept them from a nomadic father-in-law.

Bitter medicine for such a mighty man? Yes, indeed, but entirely necessary for the peculiar ministry that God had prepared for him. Leading the Children of Israel from their Egyptian bondage was not to be simply the work for a mighty man, but also that of a miracle-working God. Moses' greatness would henceforth be measured by his degree of trust in this God.

He learned his lessons well. This man who could formerly sway crowds with his oratory would complain in chapter 4 that he was slow of speech, and of a slow tongue.

The desert gave Moses perspective. No general can direct a battle from the foxholes. Generals are those who get away from the battle's heat to study maps and plan strategy in secluded hideaways. It is the general's sense of perspective that gives validity to his decisions.

To prepare Moses to be the great leader of his people, God had to pull him aside for a period of time. When in the midst of his suffering brethren, his passion incited him to strike out against the first Egyptian oppressor in sight. God wished him to see, not just one suffering brother, but a suffering nation, and that to deliver this nation his blows must be more telling.

The desert years gave Moses the time to meditate, to analyze. It gave him the opportunity to know himself and to think his own thoughts, rather than blindly conform to the thoughts of others. Above all, it gave him the opportunity to learn to know God in a personal way.

The desert completed Moses' human training. The most important lessons that Moses needed to learn in the desert were spiritual ones. However, from the human standpoint, the man God would use to deliver His children from Egyptian bondage had to be endowed with exceptional qualifications.

He had to be a Hebrew, and understand the peculiar destiny of the Jewish people. He had to be skilled in the learning of the Egyptians, to enable him to deal with the Egyptian court. He had to be a great administrator and military leader, in order to govern his nation and protect them from enemy tribes.

But yet another skill was needed to fulfill Moses' human qualifications: he had to know the desert.

Little did Moses realize when returning to Egypt that his desert experiences were not over. For another 40 long years the Children of Israel would wander over much of the same territory Moses learned to know while tending the sheep of his father-in-law. It was not easy to leave the Egyptian cities and dwell in a shepherd's tent, but the skills Moses learned in the desert were just as valuable for the future of his people as those learned from the Egyptian schoolmasters.

It may be that some Christians studying this passage of Scripture are even now passing through a desert experience in their walk with God. May they not despair, for God is just as present in the desert as in the marketplace.

III. Divine Readiness (Exod. 2:23-25)

Times of human inactivity are often times of divine activity. And in His dealings with mankind, God requires time to bring certain situations to a state of readiness. While God was using the desert years to prepare Moses, He was also at work in the land of Egypt.

1. Israel was ready (v. 23). When Moses made his first attempt to help the Israelites, his own brethren turned against him.

Impossible as it may seem, the Israelites—in spite of all that they had endured during the years of their bondage—were still not ready to leave the land of leeks and garlic. Yet when it was seen that the successor of Pharaoh intended to continue the cruelty of his predecessor on the throne, they were finally willing to cry out to God for deliverance.

2. God was ready (vv. 24-25). And when God heard their groaning, He knew that the time was ready. He remembered the great covenant He had made with Abraham, with Isaac, and with Jacob.

All was in readiness, and the curtain was about to go up on one of the strangest and most spectacular dramas of all human history—the exodus of the Children of Israel from the land of Egypt. As a result of this drama, Egypt would never again be the same, nor would the Children of Israel.

Those who are willing to await God's timing have the privilege of sharing in the spectacular.

Questions for Discussion

1. What are the marks of genuine Christian humility?
2. Does "waiting on God" imply a period of complete inactivity?
3. If Christianity means essentially letting Christ live in me, what is the value of Christian education?
4. Can you think of ways in which the Spirit is possibly being quenched in your Christian service?
5. What does it mean to be filled with the Spirit? Does the Spirit ignore our personality and training?
6. Must every Christian have a "desert experience" in order to know God intimately?
7. Is the activism of modern Christian service actually getting spiritual results?

3

A Divine Commission

Exodus 3:1—4:17

~~~~~~~~~~~~~~~~~~~~~~~~~~~~~

I. The Burning Bush (Exod. 3:1-6)

  1. God appears in the burning bush (vv. 2-3)
  2. God speaks from the burning bush (vv. 4-6)

II. The Call of God (Exod. 3:7-10)

  1. Divine intervention (vv. 8-9)
  2. Human instrumentality (v. 10)

III. Moses' Excuses (Exod. 3:11—4:17)

  1. "Who am I?" (3:11-12)
  2. "What is your name?" (3:13-22)
  3. "They will not believe me" (4:1-9)
  4. "I am not eloquent" (4:10-12)
  5. "O my Lord, send . . ." [but not me] (4:13-17)

Pettiness often manifests itself in extremes. Most of us find it easy to shift from one extreme to another very quickly. Fortunately these extremes do not always reveal the true nature of our character; few men are as bad as their worst moments, nor are they as good as their best. We should avoid making blanket judgments of others on the basis of their extreme actions.

Moses is not yet the great man God needed to deliver His people. Our last study concerned Moses' act of folly—striking out in self-sufficiency, thinking that he was big enough to do the job. Now a completely different Moses appears—one wholly lacking in self-confidence.

Both of these traits—self-sufficiency and self-abasement—are unhealthy extremes, and both imply a lack of confidence in God. The self-sufficient man forgets that God is necessary. But it is also possible to become so preoccupied with our helplessness that we forget that God is available.

Forty long years have passed since Moses fled the wrath of Pharaoh; he has grown accustomed to the rude life of the desert.

At times his thoughts go back to Egypt, but less frequently than at the beginning. Occasional snatches of news come from rare contacts with workers in the Egyptian mines of the Sinai peninsula, but the long years of absence have eaten away at the vividness of memories of his former life. He still thinks of his suffering brethren and doubtless prays for them. He has had time to repent a thousand times for his act of folly; but after 40 years, any thought of a second chance to play a role in the salvation of his nation would have long since vanished. He fully expected to die unknown in the wilderness.

Then, alone on the backside of the desert with the sheep of his father-in-law, Moses' attention was caught by the burning bush. And he was totally unprepared for what he saw and heard on that unforgettable day.

I. The Burning Bush (Exod. 3:1-6)

Moses had led the sheep to the region of Mount Horeb. This is another name for Mount Sinai, and it is here called the mountain of God. To this same spot Moses would soon return with his people to again meet God and to receive the tables of the Law.

1. God appears in the burning bush (vv. 2-3). The bush mentioned here was a small acacia tree. It must not have been uncommon for such bushes, tinder-dry in the heat of the desert, to become ignited by a shepherd's fire or even a bolt of lightning. But at most they would blaze for a few minutes, and then be consumed by the flames. But here was a miraculous event—a bush that burned continually without being consumed—and Moses gazed in amazement.

The "Angel of the Lord" appeared in the form of a flame in the midst of the bush. This term refers not to a created angel, but to Jehovah himself. In fact, the Lord of the New Testament is identified as the person who met with men in many of these appearances of the Old Testament "Angel of the Lord."

Throughout the Scriptures fire is an emblem of deity, usually conveying the idea of God's purifying power: "Our God is a consuming fire." The burning bush is a type of the nation Israel, sorely afflicted but never destroyed. Therefore, seen from the divine perspective, Israel's suffering is not simply the result of human oppression, but of divine chastisement. Men can do to God's people only what God permits.

2. God speaks from the burning bush (vv. 4-6). When Moses' attention was captured, God spoke. Only when men are ready to listen does God bother to speak to them; this is why some people can sit in Sunday school classes for years without ever hearing the voice of God. It is extremely touching in these verses to read that God spoke to Moses by name. Ours is a personal God, and He is interested in us as persons, not as things.

The effect of hearing his name called out from the burning bush must have been stupefying for Moses. He had heard about Jehovah from his mother's knee. He had certainly made a careful study of the history and spiritual heritage of his people. He had doubtless worshiped Jehovah during the years of his exile. But for the first time in his life, God spoke to him.

But though Moses was to know God intimately, he did not dare to become careless in his relation with the Almighty. "Draw not nigh hither," sounds out the warning. "Put off thy shoes... the place whereon thou standest is holy ground." One cringes at the vulgar familiarity with which some people treat God. Though God is personal in His dealings with us, the distance between our nature and His is infinite.

Then God identified himself to Moses: "I am the God of thy father, the God of Abraham, the God of Isaac, the God of Jacob." Moses understood the import of these mighty words, and he hid his face in reverence and fear.

II. The Call of God (Exod. 3:7-10)

Three words in verse 7 reveal to Moses the concern of God for His people. He says first of all that He has **seen** their affliction. The verb tense here implies that His eye was upon them from the very beginning. Throughout the Scriptures we read again and again that nothing is hidden from the eye of God. In our moments of suffering, may we remember that God is watching.

Then God states that He has "**heard** their cry." We do not fully understand the ways of God with men, and why in so many cases our prayers seem unanswered for months and even years. But though they may seem unanswered, they never go unheeded. God hears, even though He will not violate the freedom He has given His creatures, and it may take long years for God to prepare human hearts to accept His working in their lives.

Finally, God says, "I **know** their sorrows." Men can see

and hear, but only God can fully know. David says, "O Lord, thou hast searched me, and known me.... Such knowledge is too wonderful for me; it is high, I cannot attain unto it" (Psa. 139:1,6).

1. Divine intervention (vv. 8-9). God now reveals to Moses His intention of delivering the Children of Israel from bondage. This deliverance will have two parts. Not only will He free them from the Egyptian taskmasters, but also He will lead them into a "good land and large," a land flowing with "milk and honey," this latter term denoting its great fertility.

No doubt many of the Israelites would have preferred that God simply end their period of slavery and restore them to favor with the Egyptian king. But this would be to miss the whole purpose of God's redemptive act; God had to get them out of Egypt, this land which they had learned to love too deeply. Physical bondage was the result of something far more serious but less obvious: spiritual slavery to a land and people to whom they were to remain strangers.

There is really no comparison between the "milk and honey" of God's presence, and the "leeks and garlick" of the world. "In thy presence is fulness of joy; at thy right hand there are pleasures for evermore" (Psa. 16:11). Why is it then that so many Christians seem to prefer Egypt to the Promised Land? And why is it that so many of us, like the Children of Israel, must endure years of suffering in sin's bondage until we are finally willing to make a clean and complete break with the world?

But when that break finally comes, what deep satisfaction awaits us when we enter fully into His presence and experience His grace!

2. Human instrumentality (v. 10). In verse 8 God says, "I am come down to deliver them out of the hand of the Egyptian." Verse 10 says, "I will send **thee** unto Pharaoh, that **thou** mayest bring forth my people."

There is no discrepancy between these two statements; in fact, taken together they express a great truth in God's relationship with man. Moses had tried to do God's work without God, and he failed miserably. However, God will not perform this task without a Moses. God always works with men through the instrumentality of other men.

It is when we put these two statements in focus in our lives that we begin to understand our true worth in His plan for us. Like Moses, we have been called by God to deliver men from bondage, and like Moses we must learn that we cannot do this without God. But neither must we swing to the other extreme and take the attitude, like that expressed to William Carey the missionary, that "whenever God chooses to save the heathen He can do it without your help and mine."

III. Moses' Excuses (Exod. 3:11—4:17)

God's call to Moses was answered by four excuses, each rooted in the bitterness of his past experience. But only after God had patiently dealt with each excuse did Moses reveal the heart of the problem by stating his unwillingness.

1. "Who am I?" (3:11-12). The men most fit for great spiritual missions are those who consider themselves unfit. When God called Jeremiah, he said, "O Lord God, behold I cannot speak, for I am a child" (Jer. 1:6).

Yet there is a difference between a healthy admission of unworthiness and a morbid preoccupation with self. Sinful pride and false humility usually proceed from the same source. Moses had listened well when God said, "I will send thee to Pharaoh," but he had already forgotten that God had also said, "I am come down to deliver them." The Moses presently speaking is a far different man than the one who struck dead the Egyptian, but he is still a Moses who is leaving God out of the picture.

God's reply takes all the force out of Moses' excuse: "Certainly I will be with thee." To reply, "Who am I?" when God calls is like telling Him He has made a mistake, that He does not really know us as He should. Faith in God means a willingness to believe that God, better than we, knows whom

He wants to choose to carry out His plans. The fact that He calls us implies that He will supply all that is necessary for the performance of His will.

2. "**What is your name?**" (3:13-22). In the Scriptures the name always designates character and purpose. What Moses is requesting is a statement of God's purpose with a relation to the Children of Israel. For years they had been in bondage, and many were doubtless tempted to say that the God of their fathers had forsaken them. Further, some might doubt whether Moses was sufficiently aware of God's character to be their spiritual guide.

In answer to the question, the Lord explained to Moses the import of the name Jehovah (translated LORD in the King James Version), the name by which He had manifested himself when He entered into the covenant with Abraham. His name, said He, was "I Am That I Am."

There is a wealth of meaning in these strange-sounding words. On the one hand they tell us that God never changes. "I Am That I Am"—this means that the "I Am" dealing with the Israelites in Egypt is exactly the same as the "I Am" who made the covenant with Abraham centuries before. All that had intervened had done nothing to change His purpose, for His promises were based on His unchanging character and not on the changing fortunes of His people.

It is helpful for us to remember that when God saves us He knows in detail all that will ever happen to us throughout our life, and that He saves us on the basis of His character and Christ's sacrifice, not upon our merits.

But this name of Jehovah, the "I Am," also reveals the infinity of God's sufficiency for His people. Giving the Israelites such a name was like handing them a blank check to a spiritual treasure account—they had but to state their need and God was their provision.

To illustrate this we turn to the life of Jesus. In a discussion with the Jews, Jesus did an astounding thing: He appropriated for himself the same name that Moses heard from the burning bush. He said, "Verily, verily, I say unto you, before Abraham was, **I am**" (John 8:58). From the lips of anyone but Jesus this would be rank blasphemy, and the Jews tried to stone Him. But the Jesus of the New Testament is the Jehovah of the Old. And just so we will not miss the meaning of His name, He completes it on many different occasions to remind us that He is all we need. For those in darkness, Jesus says, "I am . . . the light"; for the spiritually hungry, "I am . . . the bread," and the list could be extended indefinitely.

3. "They will not believe me" (4:1-9). The closing verses of chapter 3 indicate that the deliverance of Israel would be a long and difficult ordeal. God had said, "I am sure that the king of Egypt will not let you go; no, not by [or because of] a mighty hand." More than human persuasion would be required, but after Pharaoh's persistent refusal, God promises to "stretch out my hand, and smite Egypt with all my wonders which I will do in the midst thereof: and after that he will let you go" (3:19-20).

Now Moses' question was this: Would Israel's faith stand the test? When they would again see Moses impotent before the mighty king, would they be willing to await the wonders of God? Or would they turn away saying, "The Lord hath not appeared unto thee"?

To answer this excuse God used more than words. He commanded Moses to cast down his walking stick, and immediately it became a serpent. Moses was terrified, but God told him to pick it up by the tail—an act requiring real faith, for serpents must be caught just behind their heads to avoid their bite. When Moses caught the tail, the serpent was immediately retransformed into a harmless stick. The lesson of the serpent would not be lost on the Israelites; the serpent was the symbol of Pharaoh's power. Pharaoh would be powerless in Moses' hand.

God gave a second sign. He instructed Moses to put his hand into his bosom, and it became infected with leprosy.

When he repeated the act, his hand was healed. This miraculous power of inflicting and removing a plague, which God accorded Moses, would show even the doubters that God was with him, and that God would use him to inflict and remove judgments in the land of Egypt. Further, this sign would teach that the nation Israel, though afflicted, could be restored from the misery of their fate in Egypt if they would allow themselves to be carried in Moses' bosom.

There was yet a third sign. Moses was instructed, if his first two signs were ignored, to take of the water of the Nile and pour it upon the land. When poured out, it would turn into blood. This sign, too, was an object lesson, for the Nile was the source of Egypt's life, and the Egyptians worshiped it as a divinity. To see its waters turned to blood would tell the Israelites that God, through Moses, could strike at the very lifeline of Egypt to bring about the freedom of His people.

We should note here that Moses was not expected to argue the people into believing that God was with him; he was simply to provide the setting so that God could express His supernatural power. In this age of unbelief no amount of human persuasion will make people believe that God is with us. He does not call upon us to prove His existence but simply to provide the setting, by offering Him our bodies, so that He can manifest His presence.

4. **"I am not eloquent"** (4:10-12). Moses' excuses have made a complete cycle, and once again he expresses complete lack of self-confidence. The man once mighty in word now complains that he is slow of speech.

These words are pathetic. He has just seen God perform two miracles by his own hands; yet he ignores this to protest that he will lack the eloquence necessary to move men. God's quick reply shows how shallow is his reasoning: "Who hath made man's mouth?" If God could turn a stick into a serpent, could He not be counted on to put words in His servant's mouth?

Moses must have understood the feebleness of his last excuse, for now his hidden reluctance comes out into the open.

5. "O my Lord, send . . ." [but not me] (4:13-17). In this statement Moses indicates what was behind all the other objections. In the weakness of the flesh, he simply did not want to go back to Egypt. God had carefully responded to all his excuses and had revealed His supernatural power. Yet Moses was an old and broken man. Emotionally he could not bring himself to say yes to God.

"The anger of the Lord was kindled against Moses," and yet God stooped to meet his weakness. The great "I Am" remembered that in his prime this man had willingly chosen to suffer affliction with the people of God, rather than to enjoy the pleasures of sin for a season, and God had respect for that act of faith. Viewing Moses' unwillingness as human infirmity rather than rebellion, He stooped to meet this weakness and provided Aaron, his brother, as his prophet. To be sure, Moses would have to share the glory of his calling with another, but he would also be able to share his burdens, and Aaron would go before the people until Moses would gradually regain confidence.

God looked into Moses' heart, and there saw a truer response to His call than the one uttered by Moses' lips.

Thus it is that Moses, in fear and trembling, but grateful to God for His grace and the understanding He had shown to a broken man, gathered together Jethro's sheep and began the journey home. God had spoken to him face to face! He would return to Egypt, and God would use him to perform mighty signs and to effect a great deliverance! With every step his heart burned with renewed excitement; there were emotional misgivings, but he was responding to God's call.

Questions for Discussion

1. Do our worship habits show proper respect for the holiness of God?
2. When our prayers go apparently unanswered, does this

mean our faith is not adequate?
3. Many Christians, even those who are genuine, seem to fear a deeper spirituality or a more intimate walk with God. Why?
4. Can God save men without the instrumentality of other Christians?
5. In what way is false humility really a form of pride?
6. Are miracles again needed to make men believe the truthfulness of the Gospel?

4

The Return to Egypt

Exodus 4:27—6:13

I. The Meeting with Aaron (Exod. 4:27-28)

II. The Meeting with the Israelites (Exod. 4:29-31)

III. The Meeting with Pharaoh (Exod. 5:1-21)
   1. The request (vv. 1, 3)
   2. The refusal (vv. 2, 4-5)
   3. The consequences (vv. 6-21)

IV. The Meeting with God (Exod. 5:22—6:8)
   1. A pledge to Moses (vv. 2-5)
   2. A pledge to the Israelites (vv. 6-8)

V. The Hour of Crisis (Exod. 6:9-13)

In the beginning of this series of studies we pointed out that great men have the ability not only to identify themselves with their times and people, but also to rise above them. Great men never allow themselves to lose their sense of destiny by becoming totally submerged in the problems that enslave the people they are attempting to help.

In this chapter Moses faces the first crisis in the fulfillment of his commission. It was something he would experience again and again in the years that followed: rebellion against his leadership.

Faced with this crisis, Moses had several options. First, he could become engulfed by the pettiness of the rebellious Jews and become swayed by the same changing fortunes that held in bondage his brethren. Second, he could become angry and quit. Third, he could seek out supporters, consolidate his party, and eventually split the congregation of the Jews, attempting to lead out some and leave the others.

But there was yet another option—with God he could rise to the greatness of his task. It is this that he chose.

Verses 18 to 26 of chapter 4 contain some of the strange paradoxes that run throughout Scripture, and that are so rich in spiritual meaning.

In verse 19, God says, "Go, return to Egypt"—a repetition of the command given on Mount Sinai. Yet in spite of this divine commission, in verse 18 Moses approaches his father-in-law, and says, "Let me go."

A divine call does not automatically disengage us from the human obligations we have acquired, humble though they be in comparison to the greatness of our commission. Moses could not simply leave the sheep on the backside of the desert and rush back to Egypt; certain things had to be put in order.

This does not mean, of course, that had Jethro refused, Moses would have gone back to tending sheep. God's authority supersedes man's. It does mean that those who ignore little responsibilities are not suitable for big ones.

Another contrast is seen in the curious incident concerning circumcision. Moses was returning to Egypt to proclaim God's will to others, but he himself had not been fully obedient. His second son, Eliezer (meaning "God is my help"), had never been circumcised. Doubtless his wife Zipporah had refused, having been repulsed by this act with her first son. Yet circumcision was the sign of the covenant, and Moses could not expect to discuss God's covenant with the Jews until his own house was in order. The Lord's measures with his servant were drastic: Moses faced either death or obedience. Zipporah delayed until it almost cost her husband's life, and her lack of spiritual perception made it necessary for her to be sent back to her father.

Human ties can never be ignored by God's servants. But neither must they cause compromise, even when obedience is at the cost of great personal sacrifice.

I. The Meeting with Aaron (Exod. 4:27-28)

Aaron, three years older than Moses (Exod. 7:7), would still have memories of how his brother had been saved from death—memories fixed in his mind by the constant repetition of this story. But the brothers were virtually strangers. He was only six when Moses was taken by the Egyptian princess. Whether or not the two had been together during Moses' Egyptian days we do not know, but it is almost certain that they had not seen each other for 40 years. The reunion in the desert was filled with emotion.

It is significant that the place God chose for their rendezvous was "the mount of God." One is impressed in reading Scripture to see the importance God attaches to places. All of us are deeply influenced by the places that form our past life, often more so than by events; for places etch themselves deeply upon our minds, whereas events more easily become hazy. God had used this hallowed place to talk to Moses, and doubtless Moses led Aaron to the exact spot of the burning bush before sharing with him the commission he had received.

The import of his words would be dramatized by the awesomeness of the circumstances.

Evangelical Christians, opposed though they are to form and liturgy in their worship, should nevertheless learn that weighty pronouncements sometimes require weighty circumstances. Even in our witness to others this is true, a fact implied by Jesus when He said that hogpens do not set off the beauty of pearls.

Notice in these verses that God does not speak directly to Aaron; Moses is his mouthpiece. There are two observations to be made concerning this.

First, God's dealings with men are never characterized by excessive familiarity. Few there are in the Old Testament who heard the voice of God personally. "Familiarity breeds contempt"—a truth well understood and evident in many phases of the existence of mankind. The Almighty had already spoken to Moses; for Him to have to repeat these words to others just so they could hear what His voice sounded like would be beneath His dignity.

Second, the fact that God did not speak directly to Aaron meant that his faith in God's Word had to be coupled with faith in the veracity of Moses as a witness to God's words. Thus, the force of Moses' life was as important as the force of his words.

In a cathedral in Spain faith is represented by a statue of a woman wearing a blindfold. True faith, however, is never blind; nor must faith be contrary to our reason. Aaron could not understand how God could cause a bush to burn without being consumed, but it was reasonable to believe that Moses was telling him the truth. And his faith in God's words was just as valid as the faith of his brother, though he did not hear them from God.

Our faith in Christ is coupled with our faith in the veracity of the disciples. But it is not blind faith, nor is it unreasonable faith. Thomas could no more understand the Resurrection than we, even though he was standing before the risen

Christ. But nothing was more reasonable than that he should put his faith in the Christ standing before him. And when Christ had made his appearance to trustworthy men, it was unnecessary for Him to continue appearing to all men of all generations—we have but to believe on their word to know the risen Saviour personally.

II. The Meeting with the Israelites (Exod. 4:29-31)

When Moses and Aaron arrived in Egypt, they immediately summoned the Israelites to announce to them God's intentions. The fact that Aaron could leave Egypt so easily to meet his brother, plus the fact that the Israelites gathered readily at his bidding, would indicate that he occupied a place of authority among his people. God had said of Aaron, "I know that he can speak well" (4:14).

This meeting was not with all the people, but rather with their appointed elders. To know the response of the Children of Israel, it was not necessary to poll every member of the nation. Decisions made by large groups of poorly informed people are not nearly as accurate as those made by responsible leaders, with the condition, of course, that these leaders faithfully represent their people. In large groups the least-informed and least-qualified have the same voice as the most-informed, and decisions are more often the result of emotional appeal than the result of reason.

Congregational government does not imply that each member of a church, from the least spiritual to the most, has equal voice in every circumstance, nor that all decisions must be made by the entire congregation. It means that the congregation has the right to appoint its own leaders. In many cases, these leaders are entrusted with information that cannot be divulged to the masses; yet this information is necessary for valid decision-making. The people need to show trust in the men who they have decided should be their representatives.

Aaron shared with the elders "all the words which the

Lord had spoken unto Moses." Then Moses showed them the signs—the miraculous rod and the leprous hand.

And the response was positive: "the people believed." They realized that God had seen their affliction; that He had visited them and would deliver them from their bondage. They bowed their heads in solemn worship and assent. Knowing that God had taken their cause into His own hands, they had but to follow the leaders He had chosen, and await the unfolding of the divine plan.

In the calmness of that meeting, perhaps in the still of an Egyptian night, a decision was made to trust God. This was not an emotional decision; it was an intelligent act of the will of those gathered together. They had heard the reasonable words of God's revelation to Moses. They had seen the signs. Further, some remembered other words, passed from generation to generation, spoken to Abram, their great ancestor: "Know of a surety, that thy seed shall be a stranger in a land that is not theirs, and shall serve them; and they shall afflict them four hundred years; and also that nation, whom they shall serve, will I judge; and afterward they shall come out with great substance" (Gen. 15:13-14). In the words of Stephen, "the time of their promise drew nigh" (Acts 7:17).

Soon after, as we shall quickly see, the Children of Israel would rebel. Bitterly disappointed at Pharaoh's reaction to Moses, even more sorely oppressed by their taskmasters, the masses would give in to their emotions. Moses would have to turn to God alone for the strength he needed to carry on.

But God would consider the calm act of faith shown in this meeting of the elders to be a more genuine response of Israel's heart than the disappointed anguish of the oppressed masses.

III. The Meeting with Pharaoh (Exod. 5:1-2)

It was a Moses of renewed confidence who, with his brother, gained entry into the presence of the Egyptian king. This confidence was quickly shattered.

1. **The request (vv. 1, 3).** Moses and Aaron did not go

before Pharaoh with a personal request. They stated carefully that it was Jehovah, the God of Israel, who was requesting that the people be released for three days. It was not their idea, for "God had met" with them.

Now, God intended not just to meet with His people for three days in the desert, but to deliver them once and for all and lead them into the land of promise. Why then did not God instruct his servants to state frankly His real purpose?

The only satisfactory answer seems to be that by such a request God extended mercy to Pharaoh. He knew that the king's heart was hard, and thus He purposed to ask of him no more than he could reasonably grant. To ask Pharaoh to permanently release his slaves would have been an impossible request. To ask his permission for a three-day leave would reveal the nature of his heart.

2. The refusal (vv. 2, 4-5). And the nature of his heart was quickly revealed. "Who is Jehovah," said he, "that I should obey his voice?" The Egyptian kings were haughty men, accustomed to receiving titles of deity themselves. Why should he submit to the tribal god of his slaves?

But, of course, more is involved in this request than a mere recognition of Israel's God. To know Jehovah is more than intellectual—it means accepting the moral consequences revealed in His character. If knowing Jehovah meant releasing his slaves, Pharaoh was not interested in pursuing the matter any further. "Get you to your burdens," he cries, as he expels them from his court. "Ye make them rest from their burdens."

3. The consequences (vv. 6-21). The verses that follow reveal Pharaoh's cunning against Moses and Aaron. Straw was used to increase the strength of the brick the Hebrews made. The taskmasters were requested to cut off the supply of this straw, requiring the Jews to hunt for stubble. This made it impossible to fulfill their daily quota, and their foremen were beaten.

When they protested before the king, he replied, "Ye are idle; therefore ye say, Let us go and do sacrifice to the Lord." He refused to slacken his impossible demands, knowing that their wrath would be turned against Moses and Aaron, and that the insurrection would be quickly put down.

Moses and Aaron were waiting outside the palace. The anguish of the Israelite foremen was poured out on them. They even asked the Lord, in whom their faith was completely obscured by their bitterness, to judge, blaming not Pharaoh, but Moses and Aaron for their misery. The men who were chosen to bring freedom to their people were now cursed as the ones responsible for Israel's suffering.

Pharaoh had succeeded in sowing division among God's people.

IV. The Meeting with God (Exod. 5:22–6:8)

Aaron had accompanied Moses before the elders of Israel and before Pharaoh, but for this errand, Moses had to go alone.

Only those who have known deep disappointment—who have seen everything topple to the ground around them—can really sympathize with Moses who comes on his knees to ask God why. He is not bitter; he is broken. His coming to Egypt, rather than effecting his people's deliverance, had only increased their affliction. "Why is it that thou hast sent me?" Who, under similar circumstances, has not echoed this cry?

But once again, the man praying insisted on leaving God out of the picture. "Now," replies God, "shalt thou see what I will do to Pharaoh." You have done your very best, Moses, and you have failed. Now that you and Aaron are at the end of yourselves, now that you have exhausted your resources, now you will see Me act.

And after all, is it not true that everything was working according to schedule? Read again Exodus 3:16 to 22. God had stated plainly that Pharaoh would refuse, and that it would take more than a mighty hand to move him. To be sure, the conditions of the Israelites had never been worse. But it was not for Moses to look at conditions and sink beneath their burdens; it was for him to look up, for—as Jesus would say centuries later—"the time of your redemption draweth nigh." Not only would Pharaoh let the Israelites go, but he would actually drive them from the land after God had dealt with him!

There is always such a tendency to simplify Christian service—to reduce everything to three or four easy steps. But when things become easy, do we not forget God? Our Lord would teach us that without Him, things are not only difficult —they are utterly impossible.

When Moses had finished talking, God spoke, and what a marvelous reply He gave! In verses 2 to 8 the splendor of God's person and purposes are once again spread out before Moses in gracious review. This passage is a gem for anyone who is passing through deep waters and needs to be lifted above the hopelessness of his circumstances.

1. A pledge to Moses (vv. 2-5). "And God spake to Moses, and said unto him . . ."

"**I am Jehovah.**" Have you already forgotten, Moses, the meaning of My name? Do you realize that I am sufficient for all your needs? Can you trust Me during this hour of trial?

"**I appeared unto Abraham, Isaac, and Jacob.**" I am the same God who appeared to your forefathers, for I am eternal, and My purposes are unchanging. They were willing to trust Me, even though they did not know as fully as you the meaning of My name. You are not alone, Moses; are you willing to act on the same faith as they?

"**I have established my covenant with them.**" Do you think, Moses, that this little setback with Pharaoh has ruined everything? My purposes are not fulfilled by the excellency of your performance before the king, nor are they thwarted by your impotence. My promises are based on something far greater—a covenant that is eternal.

"I have heard the groanings of the children of Israel." To be sure, the people are now confused. Their suffering has blurred their vision of My presence and of My power. Yet in their affliction they called out to Me, and I heard them. I knew from the beginning that their faith would be severely tried and even obscured, but they were sincere when they called upon Me. And I am acting on the basis of this sincerity. My purposes do not change with the changing feelings of My people.

2. A pledge to the Israelites (vv. 6-8). "Wherefore, say unto the children of Israel . . ."

"I will bring you out from under the burdens of the Egyptians."

"I will rid you out of their bondage."

"I will redeem you with a stretched out arm, and with great judgments."

"I will take you to me for a people."

"I will be your God, and ye shall know that I am the Lord your God."

"I will bring you unto the land, concerning the which I did swear to give it to Abraham, to Isaac, and to Jacob."

"I will give it to you for an heritage."

V. The Hour of Crisis (Exod. 6:9-13)

With these superb assurances Moses returned to the Children of Israel, but alas, their sore trials had blinded their eyes to the workings of God, and "they hearkened not." In this hour of crisis, Moses and Aaron would have to rise above the groanings of the oppressed Israelites; they would have to stand alone with God. Again God commands His servant to return to the Egyptian king, but this time Moses wavers. "Behold, the children of Israel have not hearkened unto me; how then shall Pharaoh hear me, who am of uncircumcised [imperfect] lips?"

God meets Moses' wavering with firmness. "And the Lord God spake unto Moses and unto Aaron, and gave them a charge unto the children of Israel, and unto Pharaoh, king of Egypt, to bring the children of Israel out of the land of Egypt."

Moses had been sensitive to the groanings of his people. Now he must be sensitive to his spiritual destiny. Not circumstances, but a divine charge, must determine his course.

Gathering his courage, God's servant faced squarely his hour of crisis and returned to Pharaoh. His meeting with God had given him the perspective he needed to pass this test victoriously. Months later, safely out of the claws of the Egyptian king, he would hear God utter these words, "I bare you on eagles' wings, and brought you unto myself" (Exod. 19:4).

Some who will read this are passing through a similar time of spiritual crisis. May they, through our Lord, be able to "mount up with wings as eagles."

Questions for Discussion

1. In the Old Testament, God emphasizes the importance of places and ritual. Does our worship reflect too much freedom and not enough form?
2. Is faith a "blind leap into the dark," or is it a reasonable act of commitment?
3. Can a misunderstanding of congregational government lead to spiritual anarchy in the local church?
4. Is there any relationship between the present spirit of lawlessness and the frequent divisions among Christians?
5. Someone once said, "True religion is found in the will." On the basis of this, is spiritual stability possible even when our emotions are buffeted by adverse circumstances?
6. Do our reactions to the great times of spiritual crisis determine God's future dealings with us?

5

God's Mighty Hand

Exodus 7:1–10:29

~~~~~~~~~~~~~~~~~~~~~~

I. God and Moses (Exod. 7:1-7)

  1. "I have made thee a god" (v. 1)
  2. "Thou shalt speak all that I command thee" (v. 2)
  3. "The Egyptians shall know that I am Jehovah" (v. 5)
  4. "Moses and Aaron did as the Lord commanded them" (v. 6)

II. God and Pharaoh (Exod. 7:8-13)

  1. The hardening of Pharaoh's heart
  2. Man's responsibility to God's Word

III. Divine Judgment (Exod. 7:14–10:29)

  1. The plagues of discomfort (7:14–8:19)
  2. The plagues of misery (8:20–9:12)
  3. The plagues of national disaster (9:13–10:29)

It is not difficult to predict what would have happened if the leaders of the liberal wing of the church had been turned loose to solve the Israelites' problems.

Some of them would have organized regular manifestations in front of Pharaoh's house, complete with cleverly worded posters; others would have staged similar demonstrations in the other cities. Labor unions would have been formed, and there would have been "sit-ins" in front of most of the Egyptian monuments under construction. Certain organizations would have been busy getting the Jews out of their ghettos in Goshen into the purely Egyptian neighborhoods, whereas the leaders of "Hebrew Power" would have been stealthily concealing weapons in strategic places in preparation for the inevitable blowup.

Needless to say, if the methods used by modern churchmen had been used by Moses, this would have spelled the extinction of God's chosen people. But Moses was willing to let God work in His way and in His time, and God worked a miraculous deliverance.

One wonders what would happen today if the energy expended by the church in politics were used to cry out to God for help in our problems.

In chapter 4, Moses suffered his greatest defeat. Because his efforts for helping the Israelites had increased their suffering, he was disgraced before the people and before Pharaoh. No doubt the Egyptian king was joking with his ministers about his cunning in so easily crushing a possible revolt by the Jews.

But had Pharaoh been able to read the future, his mocking lips would have frozen in horror. He would soon feel the mighty hand of "the most High, who ruleth over the kingdoms of men," and would never fully recover from the blows dealt by the Jehovah he refused to acknowledge.

And now, as the instrument of God, Moses would know his greatest triumph. The setting is spectacular—Egypt in the hour of her glory. The eyes of the world were upon her; her influence was everywhere. No other divine manifestation of this nature and magnitude has ever occurred in the world, before or since. Only in the end times will the judgments of God once again fall upon the kingdoms of the earth in such supernatural force.

I. God and Moses (Exod. 7:1-7)

Moses had passed the crisis. His wavering before the rebellious people having been met by a solemn charge from God, his faith was now placed firmly in the unchanging Jehovah, and not in the changing reactions of the Hebrews.

1. "I have made thee a god" (v. 1). Over and over again the Scriptures tell us that those who are willing to humble themselves will be exalted, but that those who attempt to exalt themselves will be humbled. The humble Moses, as God's instrument, would be to Pharaoh the same as God himself. His name would be on the lips of every Egyptian, and his fame would be carried into other nations.

2. "Thou shalt speak all that I command thee" (v. 2). God would reveal himself to Pharaoh through mighty signs and wonders, but Moses was charged to explain the meaning of these manifestations. Moses must carefully make known to the Egyptians that it was not he who had supernatural power, but Jehovah who was using him as His servant. To remain silent would be to appropriate for himself the glory meant for God.

A "silent witness" is a false witness. If God has transformed our lives, refusal to give credit to God implies to others that we ourselves are responsible for the change.

3. "The Egyptians shall know that I am Jehovah" (v. 5). God had already told Moses (6:7) that His workings in the land of Egypt would be such that the Israelites would know that He, Jehovah, was their God. His signs, performed through His servant, would have another purpose: to convince the Egyptians that there was one true God, and that His name was Jehovah. Israel would know God through redemption;

Egypt, through judgment.

4. "Moses and Aaron did as the Lord commanded them" (v. 6). The reluctance and resistance of Moses ceased from this time on. God had brought His servant to obedience through many years and bitter experiences. He had trained him for a special task; He had now led him to a level of spirituality which made his training usable.

We read nothing in these verses about the courage of these two brothers; such a statement is unnecessary. Each appearance before the mighty ruler of Egypt exposed them to danger and even death, and their hearts doubtless failed them for the fear they felt. Yet God did not judge them by the fear they had in their hearts, but rather by the faithfulness of their actions. Courage does not mean getting our emotions in order so that we can enter fearful places lightly. It means doing what God has asked us to do regardless of the butterflies in our stomach.

II. God and Pharaoh (Exod. 7:8-13)

For a second time Moses and Aaron appear before the ruler. The first time they had come with a simple request, and had been flatly refused. This time they reveal God's miraculous power. The rod, now in the hands of Aaron, was transformed into a serpent.

However, events took an unexpected turn. The magicians, who formed a part of Pharaoh's court, seemingly duplicated this miracle. Paul calls these magicians Jannes and Jambres, and says that they withstood Moses (2 Tim. 3:8). We are not told whether this was a real miracle, performed through satanic power, or whether it was a simple matter of sleight of hand. It is possible that the "rods" of the Egyptian magicians were stiffened serpents that would be mistaken for sticks—a common trick in Arab countries.

Whatever be the case, imagine the stupor of everyone when Aaron's rod swallowed all the others. What more would Pharaoh need to show him that the God of Moses was superior to his? Yet Pharaoh hardened his heart.

1. The hardening of Pharaoh's heart. In reading these chapters, the thing which most impresses us about Pharaoh is the hardening of his heart.

Alfred Edersheim in his "Bible History" points out that the expression "hardening" occurs 20 times in this narrative in connection with Pharaoh. Remarkably enough, 10 times ascribe this hardening process to Pharaoh himself, whereas the other 10 references say that God hardened Pharaoh's heart. (These passages are not always accurately translated. For instance, the "He hardened Pharaoh's heart" of 7:13 should read, "Pharaoh's heart hardened itself.")

When God revealed His intentions to Moses concerning Pharaoh, He said He would harden his heart (4:21 and 7:3). But Pharaoh himself instituted the process, for after the sign of the serpent and after each of the first five plagues, the text states that Pharaoh himself hardened his heart. Only when he was still resisting after the sixth plague do we read for the first time that the hardening was not simply a case of human choice; it was coupled with divine judgment.

2. Man's responsibility to God's Word. What is the spiritual principle involved in Pharaoh's hardened heart? With respect to God's Word, man is admonished not only to hear the Word, but to take heed how he hears.

On the one hand, our response to God's Word reveals the nature of our heart. This is illustrated by the Lord in the Parable of the Sower. The seed which fell upon the ground was the same throughout, and perfectly good, but in many cases it did not grow properly because the ground was bad. In falling upon the ground, the seed revealed the nature of that ground.

But there is another aspect to this principle, that which is illustrated by Pharaoh. Man's attitude to God's Word not only reveals what his heart is, but also determines what his heart will become. Hearts need not remain hard. Even Pharaoh was capable of making a positive response to the signs God gave him. But by the deliberate choice of the will, he rejected the moral implications of each manifestation of Jehovah's power.

Now, for Pharaoh, just as for all other men, there seems to be a point of no return. Thus, by the time the sixth plague was past, divine judgment had begun. Pharaoh was unaware that anything had changed; he felt that he was still in control of his will. Yet he had gone too far; repentance would be virtually impossible.

Whether the hardening of Pharaoh's heart by God was the direct intervention of God's Spirit, or whether it was brought about by natural psychological causes matters little. The results were the same.

Paul, writing in Romans, chapter 1, points out that God does not give men up until they have first given Him up. This principle is also stated in 2 Thessalonians 2:10-12. Here we read, "For this cause God shall send a strong delusion, that they should believe a lie: that they all might be damned who believed not the truth, but had pleasure in unrighteousness." But for what "cause" did God send the delusion? Read verse 10: "Because they received not the love of the truth, that they might be saved."

The church provides all kinds of opportunities for men to hear the Word of God. But have we been guilty of failing to warn men—Christians and unsaved alike—of the danger of hearing the Word without an accompanying obedience? May we learn the lesson of Pharaoh.

III. Divine Judgment (Exod. 7:14—10:29)

The word "plague" means literally a "stroke," or a "blow"; it was with these divine "blows" that God would reveal His power to the Egyptians and bring them to their knees.

The purpose of the plagues was twofold: First, through them God revealed to the Egyptians (and to the Children of Israel) that He was the great Jehovah; second, through them God brought such misery upon the Egyptians that they finally forced the Israelites to leave, even loading them with gifts to be rid of them.

This misery was not only physical and mental, but it was also spiritual. Egypt was a land of many gods, and from the turning of the Nile into blood to the darkness that covered the land, each plague struck a blow to some aspect of the Egyptian religion. Imagine the state of complete moral and physical shock that gripped the land when the Jews finally left.

There is a difference between the first nine plagues and the tenth. In the first nine, God intervenes through natural phenomena; the element of the miraculous here is mainly in the timing and intensiveness of the events. But in the tenth, that of the death angel, God intervenes directly.

The first nine plagues fall into three sets of threes. In each set, the first two plagues are announced to Pharaoh, whereas the third falls without warning. With each new set of plagues, the intensity of the suffering inflicted upon the Egyptians increases. The plagues are thought to have been spread out over a period of about 10 months.

1. The plagues of discomfort (7:14−8:19). Early in the morning Moses and Aaron met Pharaoh as he went to the river, doubtless to offer customary divine worship to this deity. Aaron stretched forth his rod, and the river was turned red, like blood. Throughout the land, even in the household vessels, the water became contaminated. However, the Egyptian magicians were able to duplicate the miracle, and Pharaoh ignored its implications.

There was a second meeting with the Egyptian king. The rod was again stretched forth, and the land was covered with frogs. Though this miracle was seemingly duplicated by the magicians, Pharaoh sought out Moses to ask for mercy, promising to release the Hebrews. At Moses' word the frogs disappeared, but Pharaoh immediately broke his promise.

Then, without warning Pharaoh of his intentions, Moses instructed Aaron again to stretch out the rod, and the dust turned into "lice," inflicting man and beast. The exact meaning of the word translated "lice" is not known; some think it was a plague of mosquitoes. Whatever it was, the extreme discomfort spread throughout the land. Here the magicians were powerless and said to Pharaoh, "This is the finger of God." But he again hardened his heart, and "hearkened not."

2. The plagues of misery (8:20—9:12). The plagues increased in intensity. At the word of Moses a vast swarm of flies covered the land, infecting the land with grievous suffering. Beginning with this plague, God henceforth made a distinction between the land occupied by the Egyptians and that occupied by the Israelites, so that they would know that this was not just the finger of "a god," but of the Jehovah of the Hebrews.

"Fly" here denotes a particularly irritating kind of insect; and since the Hebrew word "swarm" means "mixture," there could have been all kinds of venomous insects attaching themselves to the bodies of men and beasts and inflicting them with their sting.

Pharaoh began to offer Moses compromises. "Sacrifice to your God in the land," he proposed, but Moses refused. "I will let you go . . . only ye shall not go very far away." How typical of the compromises Satan offers to the Christian today! Moses warned Pharaoh about his deceitfulness; but again, after the plague, the promise was broken, and the heart of the Egyptian king became yet stiffer.

The fifth plague affected the beasts of Egypt. Horses were highly prized and were of comparatively recent importation. Asses were the beasts of burden—needed for the construction of the Egyptian cities. Camels were doubtless employed in trade with foreign countries. Oxen and sheep constituted a great part of the wealth of the people. All these animals were inflicted with "a grievous murrain," or mortal disease. Thus the suffering inflicted upon Egypt fell on beast as well as man, and the economic blow was severe. None of the animals of the Israelites was affected. Pharaoh remained unmoved.

As was true of the third, the sixth plague fell without warning. Moses and Aaron sprinkled ashes in the air in the sight of Pharaoh, and immediately boils, breaking out in "blains," or running sores, afflicted the people and the animals. The suffering was intense; not only were the magicians unable to duplicate these miracles, but they even found it impossible to stand before the king because of the boils. It is here that God began His spiritual judgment of Pharaoh: at the issue of this plague "the Lord hardened" his heart.

3. The plagues of national disaster (9:13–10:29). Moses appeared once again to Pharaoh early in the morning. With solemn words Moses warned the king of the intensity of the judgments he was facing, rebuking him for his obstinance. He pointed out that it was useless to fight against God, telling him that God had said, "For this cause have I raised thee [Pharaoh] up, for to shew in thee my power; and that my name may be declared throughout all the earth." A day of grace was given to Pharaoh. Then, the following day, a murderous hail fell in the land, killing man and beast in the fields, and destroying trees and crops. Lightning added to the horror of the spectacle.

Pharaoh sought out Moses and entreated him to stop the destruction. He confessed, "I have sinned this time: the Lord is righteous and I and my people are wicked." Again he promised to release the Israelites, but again, when the storm passed, he was unchanged.

With the announcement of the eighth plague Pharaoh seems to have lost control of his reason. The spectacle here is that of a Hitler who was willing to see the annihilation of his country rather than submit to the inevitable, and admit defeat.

"How long wilt thou refuse to humble thyself before me?" exclaimed God through Moses; then he announced the coming of the dreaded locusts. The king's servants were terror-stricken. "How long shall this man be a snare to us?" they cry. "Let the men go, that they may serve the Lord their God; knowest thou not yet that Egypt is destroyed?"

Scarcely anything was feared more in those lands than the locust plague. Even the heathen considered this as a special visitation of God. The locusts would advance like an army, destroying every growing thing, entering and corrupting all the houses, ruining the land.

Moses and Aaron left, but were summoned to return to the palace. Pharaoh reasoned with them, trying to exact a further compromise: that only the men would go and that the women and children stay. They refused to yield, and Pharaoh, furious, drove them out.

The fury of the locusts was greater than Egypt had ever before experienced. In haste Pharaoh sought out Moses and Aaron, begging forgiveness and seeking respite. But when the locusts were gone, the hard heart once again manifested itself.

Finally, unannounced, came the ninth plague, more terrible than any that had preceded. A thick darkness covered this land where light was worshiped as a god. Not only were the people unable to see one another, but they were actually unable to move about. This was a "darkness which may be felt"—that of a great sandstorm, severe and intense. The air, charged with electricity, drew up the fine dust and particles of sand until all the light was hid, as with a thick veil. The floating dust entered every apartment, pervading every corner. Man and beast alike sought refuge in cellars and out-of-the-way places, searching relief from the demoralizing oppression, refusing to move. The plague lasted three interminable days.

Pharaoh offered a final compromise. Their children could go, but they must leave their cattle. But once again Moses stood firm. God's servant must not compromise. The hardening of Pharaoh was complete; in violent anger he drove out Moses from his presence, threatening death if he again saw his face.

"Thou hast spoken well," replied Moses: "I will see thy face again no more." The stage was set for the final manifestation of the wrath of Jehovah.

Questions for Discussion

1. Is political action a valid form of Christian service?
2. Do you think that our witness in the world is giving people an accurate picture of the nature of our God?
3. What are some ways to overcome our emotional fears in speaking about God to others?
4. If God hardens men's hearts, how can He hold them responsible for this hardness?

6

Judgment and Deliverance

Exodus 12:1-42

▰▰▰▰▰▰▰▰▰▰▰▰▰▰▰▰▰▰▰▰▰▰▰▰▰▰▰▰▰

I. The Passover (Exod. 12:3-28)
   1. The Passover lamb (vv. 3-13)
   2. The unleavened bread (vv. 8, 15-20)

II. The Final Plague (Exod. 12:29-39)
   1. God's judgment (vv. 29-30)
   2. Pharaoh's reaction (vv. 31-36)
   3. The exodus (vv. 37-39)

III. "Remember This Day" (Exod. 13:2-10)

All students of the Scriptures are impressed by the fact that God records history differently from men.

Though secular historians still spend their lives doing research on Egypt, and though popular magazines still periodically run series of articles depicting her greatness, God's treatment of this great civilization is summary and restricted to its contacts with His chosen people. The glory of Egypt stretched out over a period of 2,000 years; nevertheless, in the eyes of an eternal God it was a passing glory.

The event which forms the subject of these verses took place in the space of one night; yet it is given more prominence in the Bible than all the history of Egypt. Why? Because in the light of God's redemption of His people the Passover was more significant than the glory of the Pharaohs.

Men and women who know spiritual greatness are those who have trained themselves to read history from God's point of view. Whether it be history written centuries ago in the land of Egypt, or history being written daily in the contemporary world, they seek to analyze events in light of eternity.

At the end of the last chapter we witnessed Moses being driven out of the Egyptian court for having refused Pharaoh's final compromise. But before he parted, he left terrifying words with the Egyptian king. "Thus saith Jehovah, About midnight will I go out into the midst of Egypt, and all the firstborn in the land of Egypt shall die" (11:5).

The first three verses of chapter 11 precede verses 24 to 29 of chapter 10 in the sequence of these events. This would mean that the announcement of the final plague, that of the death angel, was made in Pharaoh's presence before Moses departed "in a great anger."

The spectacle of an unyielding Pharaoh, even when confronted with personal tragedy, is a classic illustration of how far a man can go in his rebellion when he begins to harden his heart. His was not a case of intellectual unbelief. By this time no one in Egypt had any doubts about the power of Jehovah, or that Moses was His spokesman. At the end of the plagues, Moses was no longer the weak and faltering figure who first appeared in the Egyptian palace—doubtless the object of jokes and ridicule by the people of Egypt. The man who announced this final judgment "was very great in the land of Egypt, in the sight of Pharaoh's servants, and in the sight of the people" (11:3).

Two Hebrews became great in the land of Egypt. God used Joseph to save the country from famine; God used Moses to ruin the country with the plagues.

Verse 2 of chapter 12 gives you an idea of the extreme importance of the events that follow: "This month shall be unto you the beginning of months; it shall be the first month of the year to you." Up to this time the Hebrews began the year with the month Tisri, at the close of harvest. From this point on, the religious year would begin with the month Abib (later changed to Nisan), corresponding to March-April on our calendar.

I. The Passover (Exod. 12:3-28)

One should not fail to be impressed by the meticulous detail which characterizes the instructions for the preparation of the Passover. Nothing is to be left to chance, nor is any part to be played by human ingenuity. That which concerns our redemption is not left to the counsels of men, and man must never feel that he can improve the plan God has provided, or change it to fit circumstances.

The instructions are first given to Moses (vv. 3-20), who then relates them to the elders of Israel (vv. 21-28). Notice the heartening reaction of these elders. The plagues had accomplished their purpose with respect to the Israelites. No longer rebellious, they "bowed the head, and worshipped" (v. 27). The instructions God gave were followed to the letter.

1. The Passover lamb (vv. 3-13, 21-23). On the tenth day of the month each household was to choose out a lamb, or a goat, without blemish. They were to keep it separate from the other beasts until the evening of the fourteenth day.

Then they were to slay it, sprinkle the blood on the door posts, and roast it with fire. The lamb was to be eaten with unleavened bread and bitter herbs; and if any remained by morning, it was to be burned.

Two ideas run throughout the account of the Passover lamb—identification and separateness.

The preparation of the lamb. The Israelites were to take "to them" a lamb for each household. This speaks of a close identification between the lamb and the people who would share the sacrifice. Further, all were to share in the slaying of these animals. "The whole assembly of the congregation of Israel shall kill it" (v. 6).

But along with the idea of identification, we also find the idea of detachment. Though the lamb was not to be sacrificed until the evening of the fourteenth day, it was to be chosen on the tenth day. Further, it was to be "without blemish"—not just any lamb would do.

The separating of the lamb four days previously conveys the ideas of holiness and predestination. Sanctification means essentially separation; the act of separating these lambs from the others in the flock typifies the holy character of the great Lamb of God who would later bear the sins of the world. Further, just as he was "the Lamb slain from the foundation of the world" (Rev. 13:8), so were these animals predestined for their act of sacrifice.

The sacrifice of the lamb. Not only in the preparation, but also in the act of slaying, do we find the ideas of identification and separateness.

When the lamb was slain he was separated by death from the living. But after the blood of the sacrifice had been placed on the door posts, the lamb was to be eaten. It was to be roasted whole: every part of the lamb was to be included in this act. It was not to be boiled: nothing foreign to the lamb, even water, was to be mingled with its flesh. In eating the lamb the Israelites assimilated its flesh, thus identifying themselves with the same beast that had been separated from them by death. Not only did the lamb serve to deliver them from the death angel, but also it served to sustain them by giving them the strength to flee Egypt.

Redemption through substitution. These two ideas—separateness and identification—point out the essential meaning of the lamb: redemption. The lamb was the ransom payment for the firstborn of every Israelite family. Judgment was to fall over all Egypt. But God looked upon His chosen people in mercy, and for every firstborn son a substitute was provided. For this substitute to be valid, it had to be identified completely with those it would redeem; yet, for it to die, it had to be separate from those it would redeem.

Substitutionary redemption is the central theme of the Bible. From the beginning of the story of man, God painstakingly teaches us that the wages of sin is death—separation from Him with all its consequences. Atonement with God is possible only through the payment of a ransom: one life must be given for another. Those who find this distasteful are simply deficient in their conception of God's awesome holiness and the wretchedness of man's fallen state. For a holy God to welcome defiled men into His presence other than through the substitutionary death of another would mean for God to deny His own nature. God cannot destroy himself to try to save sinful men who find His wisdom repugnant to their personal tastes.

Many years after the first Passover, years during which the elaborate system of sacrifices of the Old Testament had been revealed and practiced by the Jews, John the Baptist pointed his finger at Jesus, saying, "Behold the Lamb of God which taketh away the sin of the world" (John 1:29). No Jew present could miss the significance of his words. Jesus Christ was the perfect sacrifice to whom all other sacrifices pointed. His death for men would bring them perfect redemption.

It is only in the person of Jesus Christ that we find the total embodiment of the ideas of identity and separateness. For in this one Person there were two natures. "Made of the seed of David according to the flesh," He was "declared to be the Son of God with power according to the spirit of holiness [i.e., the Spirit who separates]" (Rom. 1:3-4). Because He was man, He could identify himself completely with the men He came to save. But because He was God, there was an infinite distance between Him and other men. Through Christ, God himself bore men's sins.

2. The unleavened bread (vv. 8, 15-20). God told the Children of Israel to eat the Passover lamb with unleavened bread and bitter herbs. Further, the unleavened bread was to be their diet during the seven days following their flight from Egypt. Later, the observance of the Passover would include the observance of the seven days of unleavened bread.

The unleavened bread speaks of the haste with which the Israelites had to flee Egypt, but the fact that it was to be perpetuated as an ordinance indicates that it was rich in spiritual meaning for the Jews in their relationship to Jehovah, and for us in our relationship to Jesus Christ.

Bread—spiritual sustenance. The lamb speaks of redemption. The bread speaks of provision and sustenance. Both are necessary for the salvation of God's people. Just as the lamb foreshadows Jesus Christ, who was to give His life as the great substitute for all mankind, so does the bread point to Him who would announce to His followers that He was their spiritual food.

Many people have received Christ as their lamb, but fail to appropriate Him in everyday situations. It is disheartening to see that Christians, not seeing the present-day implications of their identification with Christ, often rely completely on their human resources except in purely religious situations. Christianity is not to be compartmentalized. We need bread daily—spiritual as well as physical.

Without leaven—pure. Leaven is a symbol of defilement and corruption. For the bread to typify Christ, it was necessary that this bread be pure. So important is this truth that verse 19 says that if anyone ate anything which was leavened during the seven days, he would be cut off from the rest of the people.

The meaning here is clear: those who allow themselves to become defiled by the leaven of the world cannot expect to maintain a meaningful relationship with Jesus Christ. We are only deceiving ourselves if we think that God overlooks our impurity in His dealings with us. To be sure, He forgives us if we confess our sins, for the blood of Jesus Christ cleanses us (present tense) of our defilement (1 John 1:9). But to forgive and to overlook are two different things.

II. The Final Plague (Exod. 12:29-39)

The first part of the chapter is almost tedious with its details. The last part moves with the rapidity of a bolt of lightning. For 430 years the Israelites had been in Egypt, and for much of that time they had suffered heavy oppression. They had called out to God in their anguish; the heavens had remained silent. But now God struck His final blow. Within a few short hours the people were marching toward the Promised Land.

1. God's judgment (vv. 29-30). It was midnight, the time of deepest darkness. Silence reigned. The Egyptians, still suffering from the depression of the plagues, tried to sleep. Suddenly, and without warning, God descended in judgment. Passing over the houses where the blood was on the posts, the "Destroyer" smote the firstborn of every household, from the house of Pharaoh down. A piteous cry arose from the land of Egypt, a cry "such as there was none like it, nor shall be like it any more" (11:6).

Some of us have lived in communities where disaster has struck. Perhaps an automobile accident wiped out a family, or a school fire snuffed out the lives of several children. The effect of such disaster, even when limited, is virtually to paralyze the community. It is impossible to imagine the cumulative effect of this tragedy when its extent began to be known.

The Egyptians were numb with terror and shock.

2. Pharaoh's reaction (vv. 31-36). The same Pharaoh who threatened Moses with death if he ever returned now sends out an earnest plea for mercy. Pharaoh had consistently hardened his heart; now God had broken it. He commands Moses and Aaron to take the people and herds and leave the land of Egypt. But there is more—the proud Egyptian ruler begs the despised Hebrew for his blessing. God had promised to deliver His children from Egyptian bondage and to show the Egyptians that He was the great Jehovah. Pharaoh's reaction indicates that the plagues had accomplished both.

The people of Egypt were even more insistent than their ruler. They urged the Jews to part immediately. God had instructed the Israelites to "borrow" (a word which means literally "ask") from the Egyptians their riches. At this point the Egyptians were willing to do anything, and they willingly "lent" (which means "gave") the Jews all they asked. This was no unjust request, because for years the Hebrews had been working unlawfully as slaves and, therefore, contributing to the wealth of the Egyptians. They had more than earned what they carried out of the country.

3. The exodus (vv. 37-39). Thus it was that with astonishing suddenness the Israelites became free men. About 600,000 men, making a multitude of nearly two million people, began their march to freedom. (The word "thousand" could also be translated "clan," making some think that there were only 50 to 60 thousand individuals who left Egypt.)

With the Jews was the "mixed multitude"—doubtless containing many Egyptians who believed on Jehovah and wanted to cast their lot with God's people.

The ragged and weary mob, their few possessions carried on backs stooped by oppression, were hardly the picture of victory as they turned toward the desert. But their hearts were joyous and they sang as they marched, for God had answered their cry.

III. "Remember This Day" (Exod. 13:2-10)

The long years of bondage might soon be forgotten in the happiness of the Promised Land, but God's people were never to forget that it was Jehovah who was responsible for their redemption. In Exodus 12:14 God says, "This day shall be unto you for a memorial." In that same verse, and also in 12:24, we read that it is to be observed as an ordinance, i.e., a thing ordained. Then, in verses 26 and 27: "And it shall come to pass, when your children shall say unto you, What mean ye by this service: that ye shall say, It is the sacrifice of the Lord's passover, who passed over the houses of the children of Israel, when he smote the Egyptians, and delivered our houses."

Thus, Moses commands the people to "remember this day." Henceforth, when they arrived in the land God promised them, there was to be the yearly observance of the slaying of the Passover lamb and the seven days of unleavened bread. This would be "a sign unto thee upon thy hand, and for a memorial between thine eyes, that the Lord's law may be in thy mouth" (v. 9).

Centuries later, in an obscure upper room in Jerusalem, after the Jews had known blessing, glory, and then defeat and dispersion in the land God gave them, a man met with his 12 disciples. The following day, when the Jews would be slaying their sacrificial animals, this man's lifeless body would be hanging on a cross, for He was the true Lamb of God. And in that upper room the Lord gave the Passover feast a new meaning; He related it to His own death to redeem mankind.

The Lord's Supper, just as the Jewish Passover, was meant to be perpetuated by His followers. For it is a memorial to the greatest event in the history of the world: the death of Christ on the cross. By that mighty act He brought freedom to all who would receive Him, and at the same time brought low the principalities and powers of the satanic world.

"This do in remembrance of Me," said our Lord; and each

time we eat the Bread and drink from the Cup, we "show forth His death" until He comes back (Luke 22:19, 1 Cor. 11:24-26).

A glance at the statistical reports of our churches reveals that a very large proportion of the members of the churches never participate in the communion services provided to give Christians the opportunity of fulfilling Christ's commands. It is difficult to know why this is the case. Perhaps some find certain elements of the service strange and even distasteful, such as the washing of the saints' feet.

But perhaps there is another reason—one even more serious—for this neglect on the part of many. Does this failure to observe what God has ordained stem from a failure to see the importance of the cross in our lives? Does the cross simply speak of one day in the distant past when we made some kind of "decision" to give our hearts to the Lord, and nothing else?

The perpetuation of the Lord's sacrifice does not mean simply going through the forms of a communion service several times a year. It means seeing the cross as the culminating point of God's history, and relating our everyday life to its meaning. It means experiencing daily purification by His blood by the virtue of His high-priestly ministry on our behalf—this being symbolized by the feet-washing of the communion service.

To be sure, if these realities—central in God's plan for men—have no real practical value for us, then the forms which were meant to keep the realities fresh in our memories will soon lose their meaning, and we shall find other things more important and interesting. If this be the case, may the story of the Passover bring us to a new vision of history from the divine viewpoint, and to a fresh and personal experience of our redemption.

Questions for Discussion

1. Do you feel that the pervasiveness of modern communica-

tions can have a negative effect on the Christian by concealing that which is spiritually significant?
2. How should the Christian read his daily newspaper?
3. Do you feel that Christians in churches such as ours find it easy to become sloppy in their observance of religions practices?
4. Can a person be saved without consciously accepting the idea of substitution in his relation to God? Why?
5. Why do you feel that the idea of substitution is so repulsive to the majority of people?
6. In what way is Christ our bread?
7. Can a person belong practically to the spiritual fellowship of Christ's body and refuse to practice the communion service?

7

The Salvation of the Lord

Exodus 14

I. **The Setting (Exod. 14:1-9)**
   1. The encamped Israelites (Exod. 14:1-4)
   2. The pursuing Egyptians (Exod. 14:5-9)

II. **The Testing (Exod. 14:10-14)**
   1. The fury of the Egyptians (Exod. 14:10)
   2. The terror of the Israelites (Exod. 14:11-12)
   3. The faith of Moses (Exod. 14:13-14)

III. **The Salvation (Exod. 14:14-31)**
   1. The protecting cloud (Exod. 14:19-20)
   2. The divided waters (Exod. 14:21-31)

Redemption has two facets. On the one hand, we are redeemed from God's holy wrath against sin. On the other hand, we are redeemed from sin's power.

This is well illustrated in God's dealings with the Children of Israel. In the story of the last plague they were spared the judgment of the Destroyer because of the blood of the lamb sprinkled on their door posts. In the story of the crossing of the sea, they were once and for all delivered from the power of the Egyptians.

In both cases, their salvation was the result of the direct intervention of God. Yet their responsibility in these two stories was completely different: in the first case they were simply to sit and wait, protected behind the blood of the lamb; in the second case they had to get up and walk, protected behind the living presence of God in the cloud.

They waited while God "passed over," bringing judgment to the Egyptians. Then God waited while they "passed over," protected from the Egyptians' destructive power.

We must avoid pushing these ideas too far in their application to the Christian; nevertheless, spiritual victory is possible only by retaining the balance between God's part and ours. We need to learn to "stand still, and see the salvation of the Lord," but we must also remember that victory is never a passive thing; we must be willing to walk at His bidding.

Though the Israelites represented a great multitude, they were not ready physically or psychologically to engage in battle. For this reason God did not permit them to take the direct road into Palestine along the Gaza strip: this would have exposed them to Egyptian outposts and warring Philistines. God instead led them through "the way of the wilderness of the Red Sea" (Exod. 13:17-18).

It was when they reached the edge of the desert that a striking thing happened: God appeared to them in visible form (Exod. 13:21-22). By night a pillar of fire appeared before the people, to give them light and to lead them. By day, the fire was enveloped by a cloud of smoke to make it visible. Jehovah, who had appeared to Moses in a flame in the burning bush, now appeared to all the people. The trying times just ahead of them would require a special manifestation of His presence.

I. The Setting (Exod. 14:1-9)

1. The encamped Israelites (Exod. 14:1-4). Not all commentators are in agreement concerning the route followed by the Israelites, and not all the places mentioned in these verses can be identified exactly. It would appear, however, that Moses led the multitude in a southeasterly direction toward the marshy area that now forms the site of the Suez Canal. The natural course would have been to cross over into the desert and proceed southward along the eastern part of the Gulf of Suez, being protected from Egypt by this body of water. Contrary to human logic, however, God commanded them to "turn" (v. 2), which meant to change their course. Rather than proceed in the safety of the eastern shore of the sea, they were to remain on the Egyptian side, arriving at a place which was a virtual dead end, with mountains before them, the sea on their left, and Egypt on their right.

Adding further to the apparent folly, God then commanded them to make camp in this impossible situation—a place where there was no way of escape and where they would be at the mercy of the Egyptians. They were to stay until the news of their plight reached the king. He would believe that they had become lost and were "entangled in the land," shut in by the wilderness. Pharaoh would pursue them, but once again, God "would be honoured upon Pharaoh, and upon all his host." By another mighty act of power the Egyptians would know that He was Jehovah; they would be dealt such a blow that never again would they be tempted to march into the wilderness to recapture their former slaves. The Children of Israel would then be free to learn the lessons of the desert without the constant threat of the Egyptians.

"And they did so." Moses obeyed, but behind these simple words we should sense the dreadful foreboding that paralyzed the hearts of those who understood what was happening. They had left Rameses with a song, but now the tenseness in the air was as oppressive as the desert sun.

2. The pursuing Egyptians (Exod. 14:5-9). News came to Pharaoh that his slaves had fled, that they were not just in the wilderness for the purpose of sacrificing to their God. It is inconceivable that he could feel that the Israelites would return to Egypt after the events of the Passover night, when the people expelled them almost with force from their midst. Yet, fantastic though it seems, in spite of all that Pharaoh had suffered from the Jehovah to whom he refused to submit, his heart again changed, and he said, "Why have we done this?"

Pharaoh is a classic example of the real nature of unbelief. Few, if any, have been exposed in a more direct way to God's miraculous power; what else would be needed to prove to him that Jehovah was God? But his unbelief was not intellectual; it was moral. He loved the world more than he loved truth. The exodus of the Jewish slaves suspended all the royal works that were in progress and threw the whole course of commerce and business into disorder. The Children of Israel doubtless represented the largest block of skilled craftsmen in all the land. Forgetting God's judgments, he wanted the Hebrews back.

Thus, imagining the Hebrews confused and helpless, he readied his chariot and led the royal army in hot pursuit.

II. The Testing (Exod. 14:10-14)

1. The fury of the Egyptians (Exod. 14:10). How long the Israelites waited in their camp we do not know. But quickly the inevitable came to pass. News was passed from one Israelite sentry to another of the impending danger. First it was only a distant cloud of dust; then the forms of the chariots became visible, their metal glinting in the evening sun. Then suddenly it seemed that the whole horizon was covered with the soldiers of Pharaoh—men trained, hardened, and fully equipped.

The Egyptian king had ordered this expedition to recapture his slaves. But as he caught sight of those despised Jews, his heart must have burned with hatred when he thought of the death of his firstborn son. Without doubt he purposed that Moses and Aaron should be slain immediately, but would he be able to restrain his passion until he had avenged himself with a mass slaughter of the Israelites? And if he could control himself, could he control his army, sick with grief from the loss of their own sons? The Children of Israel most certainly faced the threat of annihilation.

2. The terror of the Israelites (Exod. 14:11-12). The Jews fully understood their plight. But under the pressure of their testing they once again forgot everything God had taught them and reacted according to the impossibility of the situation. Their hearts changed as quickly as Pharaoh's: forgotten were the plagues, forgotten were the events of the Passover, forgotten was the fact that the pillar of God had led them exactly to the place they were, and—above all—forgotten was the presence of the eternal Jehovah in the midst of that cloud of smoke, a God who knew in advance everything that would ever happen to them when He led them from Pharaoh's grips.

The reaction in verses 11 and 12 is not the reasoned deliberation of a quiet meeting of elders: it is the impassioned cry of a mob. "Were there no graves in Egypt?" they cry. "Wherefore hast thou [not Jehovah] dealt thus with us?" "Is not this the word that we did tell thee in Egypt, saying, Let us alone?" "It had been better for us to serve the Egyptians than that we should die in the wilderness."

No mob can ever see beyond the immediate, and an ultimatum made in a mob situation should never be taken at face value. In more reasoned situations the same people would have reacted quite differently. It is even possible for congregational meetings in churches to assume many of the same characteristics as a mob, and for the people in these meetings to be ruled by the passion of the moment rather than the quietness of the Spirit. When this is the case, decision-making is wrong. Leaders must rise above the mob and reflect spiritual wisdom.

3. The faith of Moses (Exod. 14:13-14). The reply of Moses is magnificent. It is the reply of a man who has learned to rely upon God in difficult places, a man unmoved by the passions and fears of the masses.

And Moses' faith is even more extraordinary by virtue of the split-second urgency of the crisis. The words of these two verses are not the result of hours of analyzing the problems facing him, or of a long season of prayer. From the time the Egyptians were first sighted, events had to move with such rapidity that Moses' "Fear ye not, stand still, and see the salvation of the Lord," was his immediate reaction; there was time for nothing more. And this was in spite of the danger of imminent death for himself and the destruction of the people so recently delivered from their oppressors.

A statement of such spiritual greatness deserves attention.

"Fear ye not." But how could one help but fear in such a crisis? However, Moses is not addressing himself to the emotions; when danger falls, they are uncontrollable. He is crying out to the people to be men, which means to live above the emotions. We cannot help it if fear invades our hearts, but we can refuse to allow this fear to dominate us.

"Stand still." Panic was imminent—blind panic which would drive the Children of Israel into the mountains, the sea, and the desert, causing thousands of them to be trampled underfoot by the fleeing mob. To flee would be to yield to instinct, and this would spell disaster.

God was going to provide a miraculous escape, but the people had to retain order to experience His power. To stand still under these circumstances meant active obedience; it required an act of the will.

"See the salvation of the Lord." Only those who refuse

to follow the passion of the moment have the privilege of seeing God's salvation. To be sure, the situation was impossible, from the human standpoint. But to see only the impossibility of the situation was to ignore the presence of "the Angel of the Lord," who was even then present in the pillar of the cloud.

These words, "See the salvation of the Lord," are an appeal to the faith of the Israelites. They are put into the form of a command. Moses is saying, in so many words, "The time of testing is here. Do not allow yourselves to be overcome by the flesh and its instincts; actively and willfully trust in the God of your deliverance. He can save us, but it is up to you now to allow Him to do it."

"The Lord shall fight for you." It would have been folly for the Israelites to attempt to fight for themselves. To do so would have been to ignore their weakness, ignore God's strength, and suffer destruction. Faith in God does not simply mean allowing God to help us out of difficult places; it means giving Him complete liberty to act.

Paul, in a passage talking about the experiences of the Children of Israel who were "under the cloud" and who "passed through the sea," says: "God if faithful who will not allow you to be tempted beyond what you are able; but with the temptation will provide the way of escape also that you may be able to endure it" (1 Cor. 10:13 NASB).

III. The Salvation (Exod. 14:15-31)

Instants only had passed since the Israelites sighted the Egyptian army. They had cried out in despair and Moses had spoken his superb plea for faith to the people. Then, it would seem, he turned to the Lord to pray.

But he was rebuked by God: "Wherefore criest thou unto me?" There are times to pray, and there are times to act. In minutes the Israelites would be engulfed by the Egyptians. It was no time for a prayer meeting; it was time to get the Israelites on the move.

There are many things we do not need to pray about. Some pray that God will take away sin in their lives; God tells us simply to repent, which means quit sinning. The victory is not through prayer, but action, for He has already provided our victory. Some pray that God will help them love their brethren. God does not say pray for love; He says love. Christ makes it possible. Some pray that God will give them more faith; God tells us to believe. It is useless to pray when God commands obedience, for prayer sometimes indicates an unwillingness to obey.

1. The protecting cloud (Exod. 14:19-20). God acted immediately. Just when the carnage seemed inevitable, the pillar of the cloud left the place it occupied at the head of the Israelite multitude and moved to the spot threatened by the Egyptian chariots. Spreading out, it completely separated the Egyptians from the camp of Israel. Further, it became a cloud of darkness to the Egyptians, but all during the night the Israelites were bathed in light, enabling them to break camp, gather their possessions, and cross the sea in a relatively unhurried manner.

Imagine the utter frustration of the Egyptians; just when they thought the Jews were in their claws, they were submerged in thick blackness, like a heavy fog. This should have been enough to cause them to return, but their rage knew no turning back, even if they had to fight Jehovah.

The miracle of the cloud in this chapter is just as spectacular as that of the crossing of the sea—and just as necessary. Some people think that by explaining how the Israelites could cross the sea by natural phenomena, they can get God out of the picture. But how can one explain this mysterious cloud without accepting the presence of "the Angel of the Lord"?

2. The divided waters (Exod. 14:21-31). Moses stretched out the rod in the presence of the people, and at once a strong east wind began to blow upon the waters, dividing them and making a wide path of dry ground. This continued throughout the night, giving the Children of Israel sufficient time to cross over.

Soon the Egyptians realized what was happening; the receding cloud revealed to them that their prey was escaping. Their rage knew no bounds, and they entered into the midst of the waters in defiance of the incredible happenings. It was there that the Lord "troubled the host of the Egyptians." The Jewish historian Josephus says that showers of rain began to descend, with thunder and lightning, basing this perhaps upon Psalm 77. When the panic-stricken Egyptians attempted to flee, saying, "The Lord fighteth for them," the wheels of their chariots became bogged down in the soft ooze of the sea bed.

At daybreak God commanded Moses, this time on the other side of the waters, again to stretch out his rod. The wind ceased, and the waters with their destructive powers rushed in on the Egyptian army, totally crushing it. Corpses of the soldiers were washed up to the shore.

The place of the crossing of the Red Sea was probably to the north of Suez, a shallow area where now is found the Suez Canal. The fact that God used natural means to perform this feat makes it no less miraculous.

"Thus the Lord saved Israel." The effect of this mighty act upon the people of Israel was immediate and dramatic. "The people feared the Lord, and believed the Lord, and his servant Moses."

There are many believers who have experienced the first phase of their redemption: they have appropriated the blood of the Lamb and have been delivered from God's judgment. But if their hearts were known, it would be found that a good share of them have yet to find the deep peace of full deliverance from sin's power.

Perhaps they have confessed again and again their sins and begged God for victory. Perhaps they have tried to fight temptation, but to no avail.

Let us learn first from this story that victory is found in

the area of the will, not the emotions. The Israelites could not control their feelings on that memorable day, but they could control their actions. God does not judge us by our instincts, passions, or desires; He judges us by what we do. This does not mean, of course, that we live the Christian life by the force of our will power. All the will power in the world could not have saved the Israelites from the Egyptians. It means that we must, by a conscious act of the will, decide who will dominate us, the Spirit of God or sin.

Second, we should learn that victory has two aspects: man's and God's.

Victory means trusting God's power as the only means of deliverance from sin. Christ died and He lives, and His life in us is the dynamic for the life of spiritual freedom. Christianity is not a "do-it-yourself" religion.

But we must also obey. All the Scriptures that tell us that we are identified with Christ are immediately followed by long lists of commands, and these commands are not addressed to the Christ in us—they are addressed to us. The Israelites could well trust in God's power to deliver, but they had to get up and walk; otherwise they would have been destroyed.

Some people want a victory so easy that it does not require active obedience on their part. But Christ can act in us only to the degree that we are willing to act at His bidding. And when we make this step, what power is unleashed in us!

Questions for Discussion

1. What part should human reason play in our search for God's will?
2. How can you explain the fact that many people fight knowingly against God's will for their lives?
3. What are the perils of doing only what you feel like doing?
4. How can we avoid being influenced by mob situations?
5. Why does God will that Christians pass through times of testing?
6. Is prayer ever wrong? Explain.

8

Mountains and Valleys

Exodus 15

I. The Mountaintop of Praise (Exod. 15:1-21)
   1. Praise to Jehovah for what He has done (Exod. 15:1-12)
   2. Praise to Jehovah for what He will do (Exod. 15:13-19)

II. The Valley of Despair (Exod. 15:23-27)
   1. The murmuring of the Israelites (Exod. 15:22-24)
   2. The healing of Jehovah (Exod. 15:25-26)

Life is made up of periods of rejoicing and despair. When all is going well, we like to say that we are on the mountaintop. When things turn against us, we plunge into the dark valley.

In fact, it often seems that the higher the mountain, the deeper the valley that follows. Those whose emotions make them capable of rich expressions of joy are usually those who experience times of profound despondency.

Some people like to think that they will one day reach a stage of Christian perfection which will rid them of these periods of ups and downs. But this is to mistake the true nature of our sanctification. The mountains and valleys of our life are due largely to factors we cannot control: changing fortunes, attitudes of other people, sickness and suffering, even the weather.

Our Christian life becomes consistent not when we finally bring our emotions under perfect control—a thing impossible to do—but rather, when we learn to live above changing emotions. Faith can express itself just as genuinely in the valley as on the mountain. In fact, it is often in the valley that we know Him best.

The first camping place of the Children of Israel was probably Ayan Musa, which means "springs of Moses," located just a short distance from Suez. Here there are a number of wells, and the shade from the clusters of palm trees afforded delightful protection from the burning sun.

The emotional pitch of the Hebrews had reached the point of breaking. Within the last period of 24 hours they had successively been exposed to the suspense of awaiting the inevitable pursuit of Pharaoh, the paralyzing terror of seeing the Egyptian chariots, the awe of witnessing God shut them off with a cloud and open a path across the sea, and, finally, the overwhelming relief of being safe on the other side.

Their march toward a place to camp began in the silence of men and women too overcome to speak. But as the reality of what now seemed almost like a dream began to grip them, their hearts overflowed. Though physically exhausted, they broke out in a great song of praise to God.

I. The Mountaintop of Praise (Exod. 15:1-21)

This passage is a gem of Old Testament literature. The poetic genius displayed here is such that many modern scholars claim that it could not have been written by Moses. This, however, is to ignore the fact that Moses had the finest training of one of the greatest civilizations the world has known, that his long desert years had sharpened—as was also true of the great poet David—his sensual perception, and that the drama of what he had just lived through cried out for poetic expression.

1. Praise to Jehovah for what He has done (Exod. 15:1-12). This hymn of praise divides into two parts. The first 12 verses praise God for what He has done, whereas verses 13 to 19 praise Him for what He will do.

The song printed in our Bibles is probably the resume, written down later, of the spontaneous outbursts of praise of the Israelites. Miriam, the sister of Moses, along with the other women, accompanied the singing with dances and timbrels, or tambourines. This was not a well-ordered worship service; it is possible that the entire day was spent by Moses and the elders going from one cluster of people to another, singing praises to God and leading them in expressing the pent-up emotions of their hearts. The scene here is of the whole multitude engaged in disorganized and joyous laughter, dancing, and praise to their God—not a display of carnality such as would later take place around the golden calf, but a spiritual outburst of gratitude.

We should not try to reduce this poem into a neat outline; to do so would be to spoil its beauty. Rather, we should attempt to feel its emotional impact, and use it frequently as a help in expressing our praise to God for victories He gives us.

But though the poem cannot be outlined, three ideas occur and reoccur. They are expressed in the refrain, found both in verses 1 and 21.

"**I will sing unto the Lord.**" The tone of the song is magnificent. This is not the "personal testimony" of a Christian who stands up in a congregation supposedly to praise God, but in reality seeks men's praise. This song, from beginning to end, is Jehovah-centered.

Notice how this praise expresses itself in verse 2: "Jehovah is my strength." Only hours previously they were brought to see their utter weakness before Pharaoh's army, but God had used their weakness to manifest His force. "Jehovah is my song." On the other side of the sea the people had been murmuring; now these same tongues were employed in singing praises. "Jehovah has become my salvation." Faced with certain destruction if left to their own resources, they were saved by a divine miracle. "I will prepare him a habitation." (This clause should be translated, "I will glorify him.") Because Jehovah is his strength, song, and salvation, Moses' task is to give Him the glory, to make manifest the majesty of His person. "I will exalt him." To exalt is to lift up; Moses did not want to be hoisted to the shoulders of his people and paraded as their hero. Jehovah was the one to be raised high.

"**He hath triumphed gloriously.**" From the time God first called Moses in the wilderness to commission him for the task of delivering the people, He stated that His purpose was twofold. To be sure, He purposed to deliver His people from their bondage. But, even more than that, He determined that all concerned, from the Hebrew slave to the Egyptian Pharaoh, should know that He was Jehovah, the God who was infinitely higher than all the gods made by men.

When Pharaoh persisted in his hardness to the point of pursuing the Israelites into the desert, God said, "I will be honoured upon Pharaoh . . . that the Egyptians may know that I am Jehovah" (Exod. 14:4). And now, with the Egyptian soldiers buried under the waves of the sea, this refrain peals out again and again: "He hath triumphed gloriously."

Notice how this theme repeats itself throughout the song. "Thy right hand, O Jehovah, is become glorious in power"

(v. 6). "In the greatness of thine excellency thou hast overthrown them" (v. 7). And especially notice verse 11: "Who is like unto thee, O Jehovah, among the gods? Who is like thee, glorious in holiness, fearful in praises, doing wonders?"

"**The horse and his rider hath he thrown into the sea.**" This poem is striking in its perception of the human and divine elements of judgment. In verse 4 we read that God cast the army into the sea and destroyed them. Reading further, we see that it is the right hand of Jehovah which "dashed in pieces the enemy." Also, "in the greatness of thine excellency thou hast overthrown them" (vv. 6-7).

However, lest we think God unjust for afflicting the Egyptian army with such destruction, let us read verse 9: "The enemy said, I will pursue, I will overtake, I will divide the spoil; my lust shall be satisfied upon them; I will draw my sword, my hand shall destroy them." Had the Egyptians not been so viciously intent on thwarting God's purposes, they would have remained safe in Egypt. God destroyed them, but Moses would have us see that they were the ones who willfully placed themselves in the place of destruction.

The destruction of the Egyptians in the Red Sea is an illustration of the eternal destruction of the soul in hell. In a sense, it is the sinner himself who is responsible for his destruction. For though God has prepared the place of destruction, He does not force any man to go there; man sends himself to hell by his willful refusal to recognize Jehovah, and to submit to His will.

2. Praise to Jehovah for what He will do (Exod. 15:13-19). Moses did not limit his praise to God to what He had already done. Since God had already done such marvelous things, He would do others equally marvelous, and so Moses praised Him equally for that which was in the future. When we are in the hands of Jehovah—the great "I Am"—the distinctions of past, present, and future break down; God's future dealings with us are as much a reality as those of the past.

This is more than praying in faith—it is praising in faith.

Jehovah would bring fear to Israel's enemies (15:13-16). From now on until they entered fully into the possession of the Promised Land, the Israelites would be subject to the opposition of the tribes that were already there. These peoples, wicked and depraved and probably diseased from the effects of their sin, would have to be destroyed; God had already judged them. However, many of them were fierce warriors; so much so, in fact, that some of them were a match for the trained soldiers of Egypt.

It is evident that if these warring tribes were not awed by Pharaoh's armies, they would not be afraid of his slaves. The Jews, their confidence shaken by years of oppression, would be no match for people trained by continuous battles.

Yet these people would hear that "thou in thy mercy hast led forth the people which thou has redeemed" (v. 13). They would be afraid. Sorrow would take hold of them. They would be amazed. Trembling would take hold upon them. They would melt away. Fear and dread would fall upon them. They would be as still as a stone, "till thy people pass over, O Lord."

Many references are made later in the biblical account of the fear that gripped these tribes. In fact, 40 years later Rahab told the spies that came in to inspect the land, "I know that the Lord hath given you the land, and that your terror is fallen upon us . . . for we have heard how the Lord dried up the water of the Red Sea for you . . ." (Joshua 2:9-10).

Jehovah would bring the Israelites into the land (15:17). God had not brought the Jews out of Egypt just to leave them in the desert. He would plant them in "the mountain of his inheritance," in accordance with His promise to Abraham. This would be God's sanctuary—the place where He would dwell in the midst of His people. It would be the place He would "establish."

Little did Moses realize that many long years would pass before this part of his song would be fulfilled—years filled with suffering and disappointment. But he knew that it would happen, for since Jehovah had promised it, it was an accomplished fact in light of eternity.

Jehovah would reign for ever and ever (15:18). Of the three future things for which Moses thanked God, the first happened almost immediately. The second took 40 long years to happen. The third has not yet occurred, though more than 3,000 years have passed.

But here again, let us remember that when we are dealing with the "I Am," the passing of time does not diminish the certainty of His promises. The God whom Moses found to be entirely trustworthy had promised that He would reign forever, and Moses was willing to praise Him, in faith, for this fact. And though the succeeding millenniums with their increasing wickedness have dimmed the optimism of many, we can praise Him, too, that one day—whether far or near, this matters not—the "I Am" will burst in upon human history, and the kingdom He will establish will be eternal.

Thus ends this wonderful hymn of praise. Though the word "thanks" does not occur in these verses, it is one of the superb examples of thanksgiving in the Pentateuch. Before leaving it we must briefly mention two lessons it can teach us.

First, this song should teach us that thanksgiving is a necessary part of Christian experience. One of the marks of spiritual apostasy is unthankfulness. The act of saying "thank you" is a form of humility, and the thoroughly proud refuse in any way to admit their dependence upon others. Paul, speaking of the degradation of humanity, says: "When they knew God, they glorified him not as God, neither were thankful" (Rom. 1:21). Further, he says that in the last days men will be "unthankful" (2 Tim. 3:2). To fail to teach your children thankfulness could have serious consequences in their future life.

Second, we should learn from Moses' song that our thanksgiving should center on God himself, and not on circumstances. Both in times of joy and in times of sorrow we tend to allow God to become submerged in the circumstances.

When all goes well, we tend to forget Him; when nothing goes well, we tend to blame Him. We are to rejoice in an unchanging God, not in changing situations. Moses' song glorified the Jehovah of deliverance more than the deliverance of Jehovah, and as such was a sublime act of faith.

II. The Valley of Despair (Exod. 15:23-27)

Hardly anywhere else in Scripture do we have the contrasts that the Book of Exodus presents. From the joyous sounds of the tambourines to bitter murmurings: this was the pattern that they would follow until they were at least in the Promised Land. Yet how typical of the experience of so many!

1. The murmuring of the Israelites (Exod. 15:22-24). We do not know how long the Lord allowed them to remain in the oasis, but once again the cloud moved, and Moses gave the order to break camp and go on.

They went into the wilderness of Shur. This word means "wall," and it refers to the rocky cliffs that bordered the desert. After three days of marching they had found no water, and the sweet victory they had known at the Red Sea was forgotten as their tongues began to swell in thirst and as their beasts began to weaken.

Then it was that they caught sight of water. They pressed to the source and eagerly began to drink, but, alas, the waters were bitter with minerals and unfit for drinking.

To be thirsty in the desert was terrible. But to find water and then be unable to drink it was unbearable. All restraint fell, and the people rose up in murmuring against Moses. Luther once remarked that when our provision stops, our faith quickly comes to an end.

Murmuring is a sin. Why? Because it is the exact opposite of thanksgiving. This is what makes the contrast in this chapter so striking. In the first part they were praising God for what had happened to them. In the second part they were murmuring about what had happened to them. And it was the same Jehovah who was responsible for both.

The word "murmur" refers to a low, indistinct noise, such as the noise made by wind passing through trees. It is never wrong in times of crisis to go courageously to our leaders and state clearly our grievances, but murmuring is cowardly and always damaging, for it is contagious. Though the Israelites were murmuring against Moses, in reality they were sinning against God, for they were refusing to trust Him in a time of testing.

Murmuring is one of the damaging sins of the church today. It is habit-forming, for those who murmur are never content. Further, they lack the courage to face issues squarely and intelligently, and to solve problems directly with the people involved. Some churches, because of the sin of murmuring, must change pastors on an average of every two or three years; by the end of their stays, these pastors are thoroughly discouraged, and their ministry is ineffective. But such Christians are not just sinning against their pastors. They are also sinning against God. They claim that God leads them to call a pastor; then they refuse to submit to his leadership.

2. The healing of Jehovah (Exod. 15:25-26). God did not answer the murmurs of the faithless Jews, but He did answer the prayer of Moses. He showed His servant a "tree" which, when cast into the waters, made them drinkable.

Then, having "proved" the Children of Israel, and having found them once again faithless in a time of crisis, He gave them this "statute" and "ordinance"—a spiritual principle of behavior which would govern their relationship with God in times of crisis. This principle is stated in verse 26, and it is twofold: it concerns man's responsibility and God's promise.

The responsibility of the Israelites is prefaced by the word "if." If they would first hear, then obey, God's will, He would fulfill His promise. In times of testing they were not to listen to the voice of circumstances, nor were they to heed the voice of murmuring. They were to rise above all that and listen to God. Having given ear to His commandments, they were to obey Him. His laws were not arbitrary rules given to annoy them and hamper their full expression; they were the expression of His nature and the avenues by which His blessings could flow.

God's promise was that, just as He healed the bitter waters, He would be to them Jehovah that heals. Their obedience would protect them from all the diseases that fell on the Egyptians.

It is in times of testing that we learn to know God in new ways.

Many are the churches today who need to know God as "the Lord who healeth." Where people go to find fountains of living water, they are exposed to waters of bitterness. Just as it took a miracle to heal the springs of Marah, it might take a miracle to bring sweetness once again into the midst of murmuring Christians, but the principle God gave Moses is still valid today. If we are willing to heed God's Word and submit to His will, He can cure the worst of our spiritual maladies.

Questions for Discussion

1. Do you think that many of our "mountaintop experiences" are purely a result of emotional response to pleasant circumstances rather than closeness to God?
2. Must true Christianity find an emotional release in our worship of God?
3. Some contemporary worship is using modern forms of dance as a means of expressing praise. What is your opinion on this?
4. How can we determine, when we give public testimonies, whether we are really praising God or unconsciously drawing attention to ourselves?
5. Most of our praise to God is circumstantial, rather than God-centered. How can this be remedied?
6. Why does the church find it so difficult to deal with such sins as murmuring?
7. What practical steps could be taken to bring healing into situations where bitterness reigns among brethren?

9

Desert Provision

Exodus 16:1–17:7

I. New Murmurings (Exod. 16:1-12, 17:1-4)

II. New Provisions (Exod. 16:13-36, 17:5-7)
   1. The water from the rock (17:5-7)
   2. The bread from heaven (16:13-36)

Every period of Israel's history had a purpose. Their stay in prosperous Egypt was used by God to make them into a great nation; their years in the barren desert taught them discipline.

Discipline is rather rare among Christians of our generation. Perhaps our emphasis on grace obscures the fact that God's gifts must be appropriated by men, and that this requires effort and consistency.

When it comes to feeding our bodies, we spend great time and effort securing our provisions and preparing them. We set certain times for eating, and we respect our schedule. But when it comes to feeding our souls, discipline is forgotten; our efforts are at best haphazard. We forget that spiritual food, as well as physical, must be sought out, that it must be prepared, that we must be regular in our eating habits.

In this day when so many are looking for an effortless Christianity, may we remember that the words "disciple" and "discipline" come from the same source. Some of our greatest problems in the Christian life stem not from a lack of knowing the right truths, but rather from a sloppiness of life that effectively quenches God's Spirit in us. Spiritual greatness is more than learning certain facts; it is more than making decisions; it is also living a disciplined life.

The Children of Israel had camped at Elim, the oasis of palm trees and clear water. This had been a welcome resting place. Again they marched into the wilderness in the direction of Sinai. The scenery of the wilderness was striking, but the general effect was oppressive for a people used to the pleasant climate of Goshen.

As they traveled, their provisions came to an end. Their thoughts went back to Egypt with its "flesh pots." Their prospects appeared bleak. Many doubtless suffered delirium from the effects of the desert travel. Then, once again, they cracked under the strain, and murmuring broke out in the congregation.

It is easy for us, living in the comforts of modern civilization and pleasant climate, to be overly critical of the Israelites.

How would we have reacted under similar conditions? How do we react in the face of even slight discomforts? To be sure, they should have trusted in God, who was going before them in the pillar of cloud and fire. But in spite of their murmuring, God again reacted in mercy. His provision in chapter 17 was a miracle which occurred just once, except for a later occurrence many years after. His provision in chapter 16 would continue throughout their 40 years of wandering.

I. New Murmurings (Exod. 16:1-12, 17:1-4)

The Israelites murmured first when faced with Pharaoh's army. One would think that God's mighty deliverance on that occasion would have rid them once for all of this deplorable trait; but no, they murmured again when they arrived at the bitter waters of Marah. Now, faced with two new and trying experiences, their murmuring assumed more serious proportions.

We pointed out in the last lesson that murmuring is contagious. In this lesson we see that each new outbreak is more serious than the last. In the wilderness of Sin the Israelites were not content simply to state their displeasure; the "whole congregation" rose up in protest, stating that it would have been better to die in Egypt by the hand of the Lord, than to perish in the wilderness (16:2-3).

Then, when they arrived at Rephidim, a place where normally there was water, they found it dry and began to "chide" with Moses and "tempt" the Lord. They accused their leader of having brought them out of Egypt to kill them. And when Moses cried out to God, he exclaimed, "What shall I do unto this people? They be almost ready to stone me" (17:4).

The striking thing in these passages is God's moderate reaction. They were not murmuring against Moses, but against Jehovah (16:7-8). Yet God had compassion upon His people and treated them with grace. The wilderness experience was new; Moses had wandered across these areas for 40 years, but the people were unaccustomed to the rigors of desert life.

However, each new outburst of complaining assumed more serious proportions; at a later time, God's grace would cease. Paul reminds us to heed the example of the Israelites, saying, "Neither murmur ye, as some of them also murmured, and were destroyed of the destroyer" (1 Cor. 10:10; see Num. 21:5-6).

God in His grace sometimes tolerates murmuring for a time, but those who persist will know God's judgment, a judgment that is usually without warning.

II. New Provisions (Exod. 16:13-36, 17:5-7)

Moses and Aaron had called the people together, and God had appeared in His glory. They announced to the assembly these words: "At even, then ye shall know that the Lord hath brought you out from the land of Egypt, and in the morning, then ye shall see the glory of the Lord" (16:6-7). That evening the ground was covered with quail; then the following morning a substance entirely new appeared upon the earth—manna.

Later, at Rephidim, when the people suffered with thirst, God instructed Moses to strike a rock. Water miraculously flowed from the smitten rock, bringing refreshment to the people.

These two provisions, the water from the rock and the bread from heaven, are very significant in light of the New Testament, for both typify the believers' provision in Christ.

1. The water from the rock (17:5-7). Moses was instructed to take with him the elders of Israel and go to the rock of Horeb. There, in the sight of the elders, he smote the rock, and water poured out.

The rock typifies Christ. In 1 Corinthians 10:4 Paul says that the Israelites "did all drink of the same spiritual drink, for they drank of that spiritual Rock that followed them, and that Rock was Christ." Just as the rock was smitten by

Moses, so was Jesus smitten by God for our sins (Isa. 53:4).

The water typifies eternal life. When Jesus encountered the woman at the well in Samaria, He said, "Whosoever drinketh of the water that I shall give him shall never thirst; but the water that I shall give him shall be in him a well of water springing up into everlasting life" (John 4:14).

To partake of this water, one has only to drink. We do not have to work for it; it comes to us freely. Further, those who drink will never thirst again; this everlasting life will have no end.

2. The bread from heaven (16:13-36). Many have tried to identify the manna with natural substances found in the desert. There is a substance called "air honey" which falls on trees, stones, and grass, and is eaten by Arabs with their unleavened cakes. It comes with the dew and generally disappears with the sun's rays. However, it is never found in large quantities, and it does not fall for more than two months of the year. Further, it would not be suitable as man's complete diet.

Another substance is a gum which seeps from the tamarack tree at certain seasons of the year, the result of small punctures in the leaves made by insects. It has been compared to coriander seed by some, and in the East it is called manna. However, it is not fit to eat alone, occurs only about two months of the year, and occurs in supplies much too small to feed thousands of people.

The manna which came from God was miraculous. It was their principal nourishment for forty years and was supplied in vast quantities. It fell throughout the year for periods of six consecutive days, then ceased on the seventh. For five days, any manna left from one day to the next bred worms and spoiled, whereas the manna of the sixth day was preserved miraculously through the seventh.

The manna was deposited with the dew, and when the dew disappeared it remained as a flake-like substance resembling hoar frost. The expression "man hu" in the original probably means "What is this?"; this is what the Israelites said when they first saw it, and this is doubtless where manna received its name.

The Israelites were to gather an "omer" (around two quarts) per person. They would then have to prepare it either into wafers, to be baked, or into porridge. After it was gathered it looked like coriander seed; this is a small, round grain, whitish in color. Its taste was like wafers made with honey.

The spiritual meaning of the manna is found in verse 4 of chapter 16: "Behold, I will rain bread from heaven for you, and the people shall go out and gather a certain rate every day, that I may prove them, whether they will walk in my law, or not."

The water came from the rock one time, and the Israelites drank from it effortlessly. But the manna was a test; it fell during 40 years. This was a miraculous provision of God, just as much as the water, but think of the thousands of hours spent by the Children of Israel—getting up before sunrise to go out to gather it, carrying it back to the camp, distributing it, grinding it, and cooking it. It would have been just as easy for God to place it on their tables at noon, already cooked. But day after day, as they followed the principles He had established, they were put to the test by God. If they stayed in bed, they did not eat.

Just as the water typifies Christ, so does this heavenly bread. In John 6, Jesus talked about the manna in the wilderness, but then said there was a true bread from heaven which gives life to the world. When the people asked Jesus for this bread, He said, "I am the bread of life: he that cometh to me shall never hunger, and he that believeth on me shall never thirst" (John 6:34).

Though we do not wish to push the comparison of the manna and Jesus too far, it is nevertheless significant that Jesus himself made this comparison. The lessons that the Jews had to learn about the manna in order to find nourishment for their 40 years in the desert are the same that we must learn if we would have daily communion with Christ. In both cases, discipline is necessary.

The manna had to be gathered daily (16:16, 19-20). Every morning the Israelites had to go out into the surrounding area to gather their manna. They had to work between dawn, when they could see it, and the heat of the sun, when it had vanished. During this time it would have been possible for them to gather more than enough, to put it aside for the following day so that they could "sleep in." But God wished to put them to a daily test of their faith; further, with so few responsibilities, their bodies would have suffered had they allowed themselves to become idle.

Even though Moses gave explicit directions, some tried to save their manna over for the next day. It "bred worms and stank, and Moses was very wroth with them" (16:20). If they could not keep God's commandments in such a slight thing, how could they expect to keep them when the issues were more critical?

Christ is our manna. Though we have drunk once and for all at the fountain of living waters, we need to feast daily on His presence if we are going to know this life in a practical way.

The manna had to be gathered early (16:14, 21). There were no late breakfasts in the desert. Those who stayed too long in bed did without for the day. When the sun's rays shone down upon the whitish substance, it disappeared just as miraculously as it had appeared.

This would seem ridiculous to someone who has the idea that God's purpose is to make our lives as easy as possible. Why could He not have placed the manna in the evening, so that it could be gathered at men's ease and saved over for the next day? He could have, of course, but this would not have been for man's good, either spiritually or physically.

It would not be proper to make rules concerning the time of our communion with Christ, our spiritual manna. Some find it difficult to have a time of quietness at the beginning of the day. However, it is nonetheless true that "you must meet Him in the morning if you'd have Him through the day." If Christ compares himself to manna, He would have us know that we must meet Him before the cares of life begin.

To be sure, our Lord does not really disappear when the sun begins to shine. But in a practical way, the cares of each new day, like the sun, are very effective in causing our spiritual manna to disappear from our sight. Once we are submerged in the affairs of a new day it becomes very difficult to find the manna, even when we search for it.

The manna was sufficient for the needs of all (16:18). The Israelites would go out into the fields and gather the manna, then come back and measure it. When it was measured, it was found that those who had gathered too much had nothing over, and those who had not gathered enough had sufficient. Whether this refers to a miracle or to a process of distribution in the camp is not important here. The lesson to be learned is that the amount gathered was equal to the daily needs of each person.

Christ is sufficient for the needs of each Christian—and how different we are! Some Christians have the benefit of many years of Christian experience; some have gone to Bible schools and seminaries. Other Christians have little formal learning and find the Scriptures difficult. Some can gather much; others can gather only little; but the Lord is sufficient for all, if we come to Him daily. The quality of our Christian life is not measured by our learning or intelligence, but by our relationship with Him.

This sufficiency is only for those who gather daily, however. We cannot store up our fellowship with Christ for long periods of separation from Him. The memory of manna eaten the day before cannot feed our soul today.

The manna had to be prepared before eaten (16:23). This substance which resembled coriander seed had to be ground into meal and baked into cakes, or else made into porridge. As we have already mentioned, God could have given it to them already baked, but this would have been no test. In our relationship with Him there are certain things only He can do, but other things that we must do; these should not be confused.

Daily communion with the living Word usually takes place through the written Word. We can only know the real Jesus Christ through the revealed Scriptures; to talk about knowing Christ without knowing the Scriptures is nonsense.

However, just as the Israelites had to take the seedlike manna and work it into edible cakes, so must we work with God's Word in order to make it edible for our spiritual diet.

Most Christians do not get much from the Bible simply because they are unwilling to take the time to work with it. Rich spiritual truths are released from its pages only to those who approach it with more earnestness than they do the daily paper.

The manna could not be gathered on the Sabbath (16: 25-30). Though the excess manna spoiled during the first six days, that gathered on the sixth day was preserved miraculously for the seventh. No manna fell on the day of the Sabbath. In spite of the explicit instructions, however, some went out on the Sabbath to gather their food. "How long refuse ye to keep my commandments and my laws?" said Jehovah, wearying of their refusal to follow His instructions. The Sabbath day was to be kept holy, set apart for the Lord.

Now, of course it would be foolish to push our comparison of Christ and the manna to the extent of saying that there is no new manna for us on the Lord's Day. Nevertheless, the principle of the Sabbath should be preserved in our communion with the Lord—a principle made even more rich by His resurrection and the institution of the Lord's Day. The principle is this: God wishes us to set apart one day of the week which we dedicate especially to Him. Just as the manna of the previous day was eaten by the Jews on the Sabbath, so we Christians should meditate on the manna of the previous week; the Lord that we worship on Sunday morning is the same as the One we worship through the week. For many, there is no integration of the activities of the week with those of Sunday. Further, many Christians are extremely slothful of their observance of the Lord's Day. Even though the day has been changed from Saturday to Sunday, the principle of one day out of seven runs throughout the Bible.

The preservation of the manna (16:32-35). After 40 years the manna would cease. But the Israelites were to preserve a container of this miraculous food as a memorial for future generations. Their children's children would see this and know that God had fed them daily in the wilderness.

Jesus presented himself as the bread of life, but soon after, He was slain upon the cross; then He returned to heaven. Something had to be left for future generations who did not have the privilege of knowing Him when He was visible to men. Therefore, the Spirit of God inspired men to record the life and sayings of Jesus in a book. The living Word would be revealed to men through the written Word.

Naturally, the container of manna was not to be eaten; it was to serve as a memorial, pointing to the great Jehovah who had sustained them in the desert by the manna and would continue to sustain them in less miraculous, but no less real, ways.

In the same way, the written Word points to the living Word. Though we do not have the privilege of seeing Jesus before us, as did the apostles, He is no less real. And our faith is placed, not in the container, but in the Person.

We believe the Bible to be inspired of God—every word. However, we must beware of the danger of placing our faith in the words, rather than in the Word. Words are only symbols, even those found in the Bible. They are symbols that reveal to us a living Person. We have life, not because we learn the symbols, but because we know Him.

Questions for Discussion

1. Is it legalistic to live a disciplined life? What is the difference?
2. Are sins committed after several years of Christian experience more serious than those committed soon after we are converted?
3. How was the manna to be a "test" for the people of Israel?
4. Why does God wish us to expend effort for something He provides?
5. Do you feel that lack of discipline is the principle cause of an unsatisfactory devotional life?
6. What principles of the Sabbath also apply to the Lord's Day?

10

Harassments

Exodus 17:8–18:27

I. Fightings Without (Exod. 17:8-16)
   1. The opposition of the Amalekites (Deut. 25:17-19)
   2. The confrontation (Exod. 17:8-9)
   3. The battle (Exod. 17:10-13)
   4. The memorial (Exod. 17:14-16)

II. Strivings Within (Exod. 18:1-27)
   1. The visit of Jethro (Exod. 18:1-13)
   2. The judgment of the people (Exod. 18:13-18)
   3. The advice of Jethro (Exod. 18:19-23)
   4. The organization of the Israelites (Exod. 18:24-27)

God's people are frequently harassed by opposition from without and strife from within. These harassments often harm us more than the major problems we encounter, for though we are usually willing to face major problems and attempt to deal with them, we treat the harassments as nuisances and allow them to sap our strength.

Missionaries who were in the Congo during the times of crisis say that the Congolese Christians stood up courageously under the open opposition of the rebels. However, many of these same Christians fell away from the Lord in the months that followed because of the constant harassment of temptation.

The church's present state of spiritual weakness can largely be traced not to the major crises of our times, but to the constant harassment of untold little things. To learn to deal with these little things means to conserve the spiritual force of the church for the significant problems of our day. This is a mark of spiritual greatness.

At the time of the Exodus the Sinai peninsula was inhabited by at least two groups of people. The first we have already met—the Midianites. They were a pastoral tribe and were inoffensive. Descendants of Abraham, they were related to Moses by his marriage to Zipporah.

The Amalekites, on the contrary, were a group of fierce nomads, much like the Bedouins of today. They were descendants of Esau (Gen. 36:12), though they were not a part of the nation of Edom. Balaam spoke of them as the "first of the nations" (Num. 24:20); though this is a figure of speech, it nevertheless indicates their strength.

In this chapter the Children of Israel come in contact with both of these peoples.

I. Fightings Without (Exod. 17:8-16)

1. **The opposition of the Amalekites (Deut. 25:17-19).** In the instructions given to the Children of Israel in the Book of Deuteronomy we find that they were to "blot out the remembrance of Amalek from under heaven." What is the

reason for such a severe command? The answer is in verse 18: "He [Amalek] met thee by the way, and smote the hindmost of thee, even all that were feeble behind thee, when thou was faint and weary."

In spite of the mighty things God had done to bring the Israelites out of Egypt, the Amalekites had no fear of God. They resented the presence of God's people in the desert. They were doubtless accustomed to driving smaller tribes away from the drinking holes and forbidding them from pasturing their flocks. Yet the Israelites, though untrained in war, presented a formidable obstacle. Rather than risking open conflict, the Amalekites contented themselves with cowardly attacks on the weak who were at the rear of the multitude.

2. The confrontation (Exod. 17:8-9). We are not told what happened to bring the conflict of the Israelites with the Amalekites from a state of harassment to one of open confrontation. Verse 8 indicates that it was the Amalekites who finally came out openly against the Israelites at Rephidim.

But whatever happened to bring about this confrontation, It was a healthy thing for Israel. The loss of morale from continued harassment by the enemy could have eventually caused panic in the ranks of the Israelites and dispersed them throughout the desert. This could have spelled their destruction.

Christians who are constantly harassed by personal problems should learn this lesson: rather than go through life half defeated by the nagging presence of spiritual annoyances, it is far better to face them squarely and deal with them once and for all. Too many Christians allow little problems to fester over a period of long years because they are not willing to face an open confrontation. In themselves, these problems may seem insignificant, but many Christians finally find themselves driven to confusion and disarray simply because of the cumulative effect of constant fleeing.

By seeking a confrontation, we do not mean we should

deliberately expose ourselves to the enemy. We mean that when we find ourselves constantly harassed by something, it is better to solve it and be done with it. We are not to seek out Satan, but neither are we to flee from him when he makes his appearance. "Resist the devil, and he will flee from you" (James 4:7). A wavering attitude in the face of temptation will only increase its force as days go by. It takes a firm "no" to evil (this is what repentance is), and a firm "yes" to God's Spirit, if we want Him to control us.

Moses gave instructions to Joshua, a man mentioned for the first time in these verses, to choose out men and prepare them to fight the Amalekites. Moses assured Joshua that he would go to the hill overlooking the battle site to stretch out the rod of God, the same rod that brought them deliverance from the Egyptian army.

Thus, for the first time, Israel was to engage in battle. This confrontation would be different from their encounter with the Egyptian army; this time Israel must fight, not just stand by. When they were weak, powerless, and demoralized, God fought for them. But this was no longer the case; having been strengthened by God's presence in the desert, they were to allow Him to fight through them.

How easy it would be if we could just back away from each conflict with a simple, "Come, dear Lord, the enemy is at the door—You take care of him." There are times, of course, when God will do just that. But for the most part He chooses to send us into the fray, to struggle and often to suffer. Yet though we must struggle, the victory comes from Him who uses our bodies to prevail against the enemy. How well this is illustrated by the battle with the Amalekites.

3. The battle (Exod. 17:10-13). The Scriptures are full of accounts of strange wars; few are stranger than this one. Here is the scene: Joshua is marching toward the fierce and experienced Amalekites with an army hastily chosen and untrained. Moses is on the hilltop, the rod of God raised over the scene. The battle begins, and Israel, though untrained, gains the mastery. But Moses becomes tired; his arms droop. When this happens, the Amalekites prevail. Aaron and Hur (possibly the husband of Miriam, if Jewish tradition is true) find a stone for him to sit on, and one on either side they hold his arms aloft. Israel gains the victory.

Here, then, was a war won by two armies. There was the visible army led by Joshua, but there was also an invisible army which fought through the intercession of Moses. Though God used real people to combat the enemy, the victory was achieved by the presence of an army the enemy could not see. One is reminded of the story of Elisha and the Syrian army, where "the Lord opened the eyes of the young man, and he saw, and behold the mountain was full of the horses and chariots of fire round about Elisha" (2 Kings 6:17).

4. The memorial (Exod. 17:14-16). After the battle God instructed Moses to write an account of the battle in a book, and also to rehearse it in the ears of Joshua, who would in the future need to remember that God was responsible for the Jewish victories. Moses built an altar to the Lord and called it "Jehovah-nissi," the Lord my banner. Israel had fought under the banner of Jehovah. What rejoicing there must have been on that day!

Because this account has been preserved in "the Book," we can profit from the lessons of that memorable war. Let us briefly mention three of these.

First, this war illustrates the fine balance between the human and the divine in God's work among men. This has already been seen on other occasions in our study of Exodus. Most of our mistaken interpretations about the Christian life and victory do not come from untruths, but from failing to see all the truth. Some people, when faced with a spiritual problem, leave God completely out of the picture. Others think that to be identified with Christ means that they themselves are completely out of the picture, that Christ has completely replaced them. You can find Scripture texts to bolster both sides of the argument, but the truth comes when you put them all together and see the marvelous balance between God's part and man's, as is seen in this battle.

Second, in view of this balance between the human and the divine, the church should mobilize her forces accordingly, in order to fight God's battles in God's way. Joshua might have wanted to be up there on the mountain holding the rod, but his place was with the army. Moses might have preferred being in the heat of the battle, but had he gone, they would have been defeated. Aaron and Hur were just as important holding up his arms as the soldiers wielding the spears. Because Moses had mobilized his forces to utilize both the human and the divine, victory was won.

How many churches are organized in a conscious effort to channel God's power through the church functions? To be sure, we have our prayer meetings, but most generally the prayer meeting is one thing, the other activities are another, and the twain scarcely meet. We love to squeeze everyone into the same mold: to create Mr. Ideal Christian, who spends a prescribed amount of time in prayer, in Bible study, and in witnessing, regardless of what his gifts may be. Most Christians are frustrated because their weak points do not measure up to the strong points of their brethren, and vice versa. Few seem able to find a true sense of value by conformity to the person of Christ, for they are too busy trying to conform to someone else.

Few things are more needed in today's churches than a good pruning of useless branches and leaves that will only be thrown into the fire at harvest time, and a restructuring of the church to allow the force of the vine to flow freely through the branches in order to produce genuine fruit.

Third, this story of the war with the Amalekites illustrates the absolute necessity of intercession in God's battles. When the arms were uplifted, Israel prevailed; when they fell, the enemy gained.

We are told to pray without ceasing. This does not mean pray all day long, or maintain a constant attitude of prayer.

Such is impossible. It means to pray without quitting. In other words, pray until the victory is won—not just once or twice, then forget.

Many Christians wonder why they should continue to pray about things since God does not forget. The answer is in this story. Though God lives in eternity, men live in time, and we are men. It takes time for God to work out His purposes in the lives of men, for they do not always cooperate. For a reason we cannot know, God has chosen not to work when His people do not intercede. What a tragedy to pray for years—during which God is working in unseen ways to bring about the answer—then to give up and forget. Moses' intercession was just as needed when his arms were tired as at the beginning of the battle. May the church seek ways to keep the arms of God's people lifted toward Him.

II. Strivings Within (Exod. 18:1-27)

The second part of our lesson is entirely different from the first, but it still concerns harassment. Here, the harassment comes from within the camp of Israel.

1. The visit of Jethro (Exod. 18:1-13). The Children of Israel left Rephidim to camp at the "mount of God," where Moses had formerly pastured the flocks of Jethro. News travels fast in nomadic countries, and so when Jethro learned of Moses' return, he brought him his wife and two sons. After the typical Oriental greetings, Moses related to his father-in-law all that God had done since his departure, and Jethro rejoiced, saying, "Now I know that Jehovah is greater than all gods." The priest of Midian offered sacrifices to Jehovah and joined in breaking bread with Aaron and the elders of Israel.

2. The judgment of the people (Exod. 18:13-18). The following day Moses sat to judge the people, and from morning to evening he heard their complaints and revealed to them God's will. The Jews were a stiff-necked people, and this vast multitude was constantly harassed by internal strivings. God had not yet revealed His laws to them, and so to have a semblance of order they had to line up and file before Moses, God's representative, who would patiently hear them out and interpret to them God's will.

To be sure, this was an impossible task. Jethro was amazed. "The thing that thou doest is not good," said he. "Thou wilt surely wear away, both thou, and this people that is with thee; for this thing is too heavy for thee; thou art not able to perform it thyself alone" (vv. 17-18).

Here, then, was harassment of a different sort—the harassment of continual little problems that in themselves were not overly important but that risked, by the weight of their multiplicity, to neutralize Moses' effectiveness as the leader of the Jews. And because it was humanly impossible for him to deal with all the problems, there was the risk of eventual anarchy, the people not having any absolute values to guide them in settling their differences.

3. The advice of Jethro (Exod. 18:19-23). Jethro's advice was in three parts.

a. "Be thou for the people to God-ward, that thou mayest bring the causes to God." This rather heavy translation simply means that Moses was to be the mediator between the people and God, to bring their affairs before Jehovah.

b. "Thou shalt teach them ordinances and laws, and shalt shew them the way wherein they must walk, and the work that they must do." In other words, Moses was not to spend his time dealing individually with every problem, but to teach the people general principles of right and wrong, so that they could make their own applications.

c. "Moreover thou shalt provide out of all the people able men, such as fear God, men of truth, hating covetousness, and place such over them, to be rulers of thousands, and rulers of hundreds, rulers of fifties and rulers of tens." Theirs was to be neither a monarchy nor anarchy, but a form of government in which there would be absolute values proceeding from an absolute God, applied to the people by trustworthy men, who in turn were subject to men over them. Little cases would be dealt with quickly by the rulers of tens; harder cases would be referred higher up. Relatively few cases would finally reach Moses, and his time would be spent seeking God's will and in revealing God's will to the people through their chosen leaders.

4. The organization of the Israelites (Exod. 18:24-27). The conversation of Moses and Jethro was not like the typical committee meeting of today where problems are discussed and solutions are proposed, after which all continues unchanged and talk gradually becomes more important than action. Moses saw the wisdom of Jethro's advice and was willing to implement it by calling for a complete restructuring of the congregation of Israel.

We should make two observations concerning Jethro's advice.

First, though Christians are not to conform to the world, they can nevertheless profit from the wisdom of the world. Moses did not haughtily refuse the advice of Jethro just because the latter was not of the Jewish race. Truth is truth, wherever it is found, and Jesus said that the children of the world are wiser in their generation than the children of light.

The note in the Scofield Bible which criticizes Moses' action here is unjustified; verse 23 implies that Moses probably sought God's will before putting this practice into operation, and there is no evidence that it was quickly abandoned. The Scriptures present us with absolute principles in the organization of God's work, but they allow great flexibility in the application of these principles to changing situations and cultures. To traditionalize the methods that fit our culture and generation and to attempt to preserve them unchanged for every other culture and generation is to risk doing violence to the very principles that brought them into being.

The church's effectiveness and outreach could be vastly increased by the application of sound principles. Especially is this true in missions. One strategist estimates that missions could increase their effectiveness by 100 percent without even adding one missionary on the fields, simply by solving some basic problems of organization. No business could make profits if it had to operate under the same handicaps as many missionary organizations, where either strategy remains undefined, or else missionaries choose to ignore the strategy agreed upon by the group, with no fear of dismissal or discipline.

Second, these principles, though proposed by a nomad who lived in the desert over 3,000 years ago, are just as valid for us today as they were for Moses. In fact, there is a striking resemblance between the words of Jethro and the words of the apostles in the New Testament.

The apostles refused to get involved in the squabbles between the Jewish and Gentile widows, saying that they had other things to do—prayer and the ministry of the Word. This did not mean that the widows' squabbles should be ignored; deacons were appointed to deal with these problems. It does mean that the men appointed to minister the Word would do well if they left the petty strivings to others appointed to deal with them. For the spiritual leaders to submerge themselves in a sea of mundane matters exposes them to two dangers: the danger of becoming trivial by neglecting the weighty matters in favor of the petty, and the danger of becoming so involved in little things that their ministry is profaned in the eyes of the people.

In our system of congregational government a church undergoes an almost total upheaval with each change of pastor. Is this because we have misunderstood the true nature of congregational government? The church which is willing to place more responsibility in the hands of designated people, provided that these people possess the spiritual qualifications, will be the church which will develop spiritual greatness in lives, and at the same time prevent its leaders from becoming harassed with pettiness.

Questions for Discussion

1. Were the Amalekites justified in opposing the Israelites?
2. Are personality problems in the church the result of a refusal to deal with annoyances frankly when they arise?
3. What personal lessons can we learn from Moses' uplifted hands in the battle with the Amalekites?
4. Is the church of today overwhelmed by things that do not have eternal value?
5. To what extent can the church allow itself to be influenced by the world?

II

The Will of Jehovah

Exodus 19—20

▲▲▲▲▲▲▲▲▲▲▲▲▲▲▲▲▲▲▲▲▲▲▲▲▲▲▲▲▲▲

I. **The Preparation of the People (Exod. 19)**

   1. Consecration (vv. 3-9)
   2. Purification (vv. 10-15)
   3. Reverence (vv. 16-25)

II. **The Giving of the Law (Exod. 20:1-17)**

   1. The basis for the Law (vv. 1-2)
   2. The meaning of the Law (vv. 3-17)

III. **The Construction of the Altar (Exod. 20:18-26)**

   1. The fear of the people (vv. 19-21)
   2. The response of God (vv. 22-26)

One of the more obvious characteristics of our generation is our changing attitude toward law. Law is no longer considered something absolute, to be used to mold society, but something that must be molded by society and its changing needs. When one leaves the circles of biblical Christianity, he quickly learns that rare are the individuals who still believe that the moral law of God is a valid standard for behavior under all circumstances. The advocates of situation ethics would have us to believe that each situation must be allowed to formulate its own principles.

There have always been sinners, but in a previous age, when black was black and white was white, those who ignored God's standards of morality were called transgressors of the Law. This is no longer the case; today all is an undefinable gray.

It is evident that Christians need to give much more attention to the question of Law. To say that we are under grace does not mean that we can ignore these weighty chapters and their implications. The man who ignores God's standards cannot know spiritual greatness.

We come in this chapter to the high point of the desert experience—Sinai. F. B. Meyer says in his notes on Exodus, "So far in the history of the world nothing has happened with the single exception of Bethlehem and Calvary, so august, so momentous, so sublime as the giving of the Law of God at Sinai."

God's history of the redemption of the human race centers around several pivotal events, and this is certainly one of the greatest. For here God revealed in detail, in a way unique in history, His will for His people. And in revealing His will, He revealed His character.

I. The Preparation of the People (Exod. 19)

The scene described by this chapter is awesome. Moses goes between God and the people, acting as the mediator. Through Moses, God gives instructions to the people. Then, on the third day, God speaks, in the midst of terrifying physical disturbances.

1. Consecration (vv. 3-9). As we have seen so many times, God does not bother to speak to people who are not willing to listen. Before revealing His Law, He exacts a promise of obedience in the form of a covenant, an agreement made between two parties, binding both by certain rights and obligations.

"Ye have seen what I did." Faith in God is never an empty thing. We have confidence in God's promises for the future because He has proved himself faithful in so many ways in the past. The same God who had wrought such great victory over the Egyptians could be counted upon to continue to work in the same miraculous ways.

"If ye will obey my voice." God is able, but He will not work against the will of His people. Obedience to God's will provides the avenues between God and man to allow God's blessings to flow to them.

"Then ye shall be. . . ." God gives His people a threefold promise if they will fulfill their part of the covenant. First, He promises that they will be a peculiar treasure to Him, above all people. This denotes ownership, and it is this ownership which gives value. Value is not measured by the intrinsic worth of a thing; it is measured by its worth to its owner. We find our true value not in ourselves, but in the fact that we have been chosen by God.

Second, God promises that they will be a kingdom of priests. This conveys the thought of channeling the blessings of God to others. That which they receive from God is to be made available to all mankind, for its good.

Third, God promises that they will be a holy nation. To be holy means to be separated: separated to God from the other nations of the earth. But Edersheim points out that this meaning is secondary. The primary meaning of holiness, says he, is to be "splendid, beautiful, pure and uncontaminated." By dwelling in the light of God's glory, Israel would share this glory, and in this way bring glory to the world.

The words of this covenant are almost duplicated by Peter in 1 Peter 2:9: "Ye are a chosen generation, a royal priesthood, an holy nation, a peculiar people; that he should shew forth the praises of him who hath called you out of darkness into his marvellous light."

2. Purification (vv. 10-15). In the preceding verses holiness was a promise. Here it is a command. Before hearing God speak, the people had to purify themselves. This purification was to be inner, of course, but it had to be symbolized by outer observances—the washing of the clothes, the abstinence from sexual relations.

Above all, this sanctification was represented by setting bounds between God and the people. God would come down to the people on the mount, but they were strictly forbidden to go beyond the bounds and touch the mountain. Whoever would ignore this commandment would be put to death.

3. Reverence (vv. 16-25). On the third day the people were prepared to meet Jehovah. They had given their promise of obedience. They had purified themselves. In the morning of that fearful day a thick cloud descended upon the mountain, and from this cloud came lightnings and thunder that reverberated across the plains and seemed to shake even the mountains. A trumpet sounded, and the people in the camp trembled for fear. Moses assembled the people at the base of the fiery, quaking mountain. The eerie sound of the trumpet became louder and louder, until the emotions of the people seemed stretched to the breaking point. Then it was that Moses, gathering his courage, spoke out to Jehovah in the cloud, and Jehovah answered by an audible voice in the hearing of the people. This is doubtless the only occasion in history that the voice of God was heard by such a great multitude. Because they heard His voice, they would know beyond doubt that the Law He was about to give was not of human fabrication, and that Moses was His representative to bring this Law to the people.

Jehovah called Moses into the cloud, then sent him back to warn the people again not to let their curiosity tempt them to follow him. Even the priests must remain without. Only Aaron was to accompany Moses behind the veil of the smoke into His presence.

Thus, in this dramatic way, God exacted reverence from His people. They were not to take His presence lightly, nor His commands. These words seem strange and almost unreasonable when we compare them with the casual manner by which most of us try to worship God. To be sure, we can come boldly to the throne of grace, seeing we have a Great High Priest who has given us access to the very presence of God. But to come boldly is never to come irreverently, and many worship services are worship in name only.

II. The Giving of the Law (Exod. 20:1-17)

Christians in Brethren churches tend to give little attention to chapters such as this. We are not under Law, but under grace, and so we relegate the Ten Commandments to another dispensation and find little personal value in their study. How many Brethren children can recite the Ten Commandments by heart, as is true in many other denominations?

It is true that we are no longer under Law. But it is also true that the Law has an eternal quality, because it is given by an eternal God. The Law can never make us righteous, but it is nevertheless the will of God that the righteousness of the Law be fulfilled in us (Rom. 8:4). To ignore God's Law is to ignore the real purpose of grace. We are dead to the Law, but the Law is not dead. And we are dead to the Law only because we are united to Christ, whose absolute standard of righteousness makes written rules irrelevant.

In our churches one sometimes discovers a defective attitude toward law in general, and this is alarming. This is, of course, not the fault of emphasizing the biblical doctrine of grace; it is the result of not seeing grace in its complete expression. This defective attitude toward law can cause Christians to become lax in their moral obligations, evidently because they feel they are in a more favored position with God than ordinary mortals. When businessmen are loath to deal with Christians because they have been stung too many times, we have reached a sorry state of affairs.

1. The basis for the Law (vv. 1-2). Before telling His people what they should do, God told them who He was: "I am Jehovah thy God." He had redeemed them by bringing them out of their bondage; therefore, they were to be obedient to His commands.

The force of a command is relative to the authority of its author. A 10 year old is good at giving commands to his younger brothers and sisters, and often these commands are as good as the ones given by the parents. But few children listen to their 10-year-old brothers or sisters, in spite of their eloquence. Mother or Dad can state the same command in simple terms, and if they have taught their children the meaning of parental authority, the children will readily obey.

Absolute law finds its force only in an absolute God. Any moral system based on less than this quickly breaks down. Psalm 14 begins by saying, "The fool hath said in his heart, there is no God." It continues with these words: "They are corrupt, they have done abominable works, there is none that doeth good." In Romans 1, the process of degeneration began when men changed the glory of the incorruptible God into an image made like corruptible man.

The present wave of lawlessness in the United States is the inevitable result of our country's rejection of a personal, absolute God who has a right to regulate the affairs of men because He has created them. If man has evolved from lower forms of life, where can one find a basis for morality? Democracy can only function permanently when men believe in a higher power. This country will continue on its road toward anarchy either until we return to our original submission to God, or else until some man takes the place of God and sets himself up as an absolute ruler here on earth. Anarchy either destroys or leads to a dictatorship of one kind or another.

2. The meaning of the Law (vv. 3-17). It is not our purpose in this chapter to discuss the Ten Commandments in detail, but to make two observations that should enrich our appreciation of them.

First, the commandments are a revelation of God's nature. Some people have a strange idea about law: they think of it as something entirely arbitrary, having no real relationship either to the one who invents it or the one who has to submit to it. They picture God sitting in heaven thinking up a set of rules that He forces His people to obey.

You see this everywhere. Pick up some of the books written for couples contemplating marriage. The reasoning is like this: if your church forbids premarital relations, by all means avoid them. But if not, there is no harm. In other words, if you do not accept the Christian's God, you do not have to accept the Christian's rules.

This view of law misses completely its meaning. God's Laws are not arbitrary—something people with the Judeo-Christian heritage are bound to, but which everyone else can ignore. God's Law is the expression of His nature; it is His will. And because it is the expression of His nature, it is the expression of man's nature as well, for man is His creature. No one could ever really abolish the Law without abolishing God himself. Further, to try to release man from the Law is to lead him to self-destruction.

All efforts to throw off moral law lead to man's ruin, for though man may reject God, he is still a creature of God and is forced to live in God's world, a world which is designed to function according to God's laws. Even the man who claims to be so sophisticated that he will permit anything gets jealous when someone steals his wife.

Even a casual reading of the Ten Commandments shows how this is true. The first four concern man's relation to God; the rest concern man's relationship to fellow man. The God who made us ought to be better qualified than we to know how we can best function; His commandments are a prescription for the kind of life we were designed to live.

The intimate connection between the Law and the nature of God and man is illustrated by Jesus' commandments on the Law. He said that the whole Law was summed up by love to God and love to fellow man. The commandments, therefore, are so natural that if we have perfect love we do not need them; we will do automatically what they command. This, however, is not the same as the so-called "new morality," which says that love can permit us to do things that the Law forbids. We need to test our love by looking at the commandments. If love tells us to do anything that God's written Law forbids, then we can be sure that something is defective about our love. The only safe way of accepting situation ethics is to allow God to have the liberty of judging the situation. He sees situations in their eternal context, not from the passion of an embrace in the back seat of a car. If He says that some things are wrong in every situation, let us be willing to admit that He knows more about us than we do.

Second, the Law has a liberating as well as a restraining element. The common view of law is that of restraint. Many psychologists, recognizing the devastating effect of guilt on the human personality, try to abolish guilt by abolishing law. How ignorant they are of man's true nature! Inhibitions are not a result of law, but of man's perverted nature, which only Christ can correct. The present wave of moral looseness has provoked a deluge of psychological disorders unknown in strict, puritanical America. How long will so-called scientific men continue to ignore evidence in the area of morals!

It is true that law has a restraining effect, and that men frequently chafe under its demands. This is true of society as a whole; it is also true of individuals. But because law is so closely bound to the nature of God and man, it also has a liberating element. This liberating element of the Law is often seen in the Old Testament passages, such as Psalm 119, in which David writes the longest chapter of the Bible to extoll the Law and to exclaim how much he loves it.

When a scientist discovers a physical law, it brings great joy, for it provides him the liberty of using this as a channel to achieve his goal. God's Law can be seen in the same way. The Law of God is like the wires which channel electric force to places where it can be used and appreciated. Electricity is ever seeking to escape the restraint of these channels, and when it does, it not only dissipates its force but can also cause great tragedy.

Yes, let us avoid legalism; we are not under the old dispensation. But at the same time, let us combat lawlessness, both in self and in society. There is nothing wrong with the Law. Paul says that it is "holy, just, and good." He tells us, "I delight in the law of God" (Rom. 7:12, 22). The problem is with us—and here is the source of all the frustration. To find freedom is not to throw off the Law; it is to find victory in Christ.

III. The Construction of the Altar (Exod. 20:18-26)

1. The fear of the people (vv. 19-21). The sight of the smoking mountain and the sound of God's voice were more than the people could bear. Rather than approach Him, they drew back and stood far off. To Moses they said, "Speak thou with us and we will hear, but let not God speak with us, lest we die." How different is this scene from the touching incident of the New Testament where Jesus called the children to himself—how different the old covenant from the new! And yet both are necessary if man is to know God. We can really know the Jesus of love and grace only after we learn to know the Jehovah of law and judgment. They are one and the same.

2. The response of God (vv. 22-26). Though the Israelites might fear the reality and awesomeness of the true God, they must never make for themselves a false one, one that might be easier to please. Rather, Moses was to construct an altar upon which sacrifices would be offered, thus allowing sinful man to approach the holy God.

Just as you can never abolish Law in the dispensation of grace, so can you never abolish grace in the dispensation of Law. The Children of Israel could not live without God, but none of them would ever be able to approach Him on the basis of their righteousness. The Law would reveal their sinfulness, but it could not make them just.

Along with the Law, there must always be the altar, until the day that the spotless Lamb of God himself would once and for all provide access to God by His death on the cross.

Questions for Discussion

1. Is God's covenant with the Christian conditional on the Christian's obedience?
2. Can a person be obedient to God's Laws and still not be holy in the biblical sense?
3. Do you think that low standards of reverence for the Person of God influence our attitude toward God's laws?
4. What is the Christian freedom about which Paul talks in Galatians?
5. The legalism of the Pharisees was seen in their rejection of the real Law of God and their slavery to man-made ordinances. Can this tendency be seen in Christianity today?
6. Why is it possible for the pagans to do by nature the things written in the Law?
7. Why can Law never be separated from grace?

12

A Rebellious People

Exodus 24, 32

I. The Ratification of the Covenant (Exod. 24)
   1. The promise of obedience (vv. 3, 7)
   2. The blood of the covenant (vv. 4-6, 8)
   3. The vision of God (vv. 9-11)
   4. Moses in the mountain (vv. 12-18)

II. The Folly of the Israelites (Exod. 32)
   1. The construction of the golden calf (vv. 1-6)
   2. The intercession of Moses (vv. 7-14)
   3. Moses' wrath (vv. 19-24)
   4. The judgment of the rebellious (vv. 25-29)
   5. Moses and God (vv. 30-35)

The theme of this book has been spiritual greatness, and for the most part this theme has been developed from incidents in the life of Moses. Thus far we have covered the text rather carefully, but now we must omit two sections of Exodus because they do not relate directly to our theme.

The first section is chapters 21 through 23, which contain a detailed list of ordinances which were to regulate the life of Israel: laws relating to civil rights, property, morals, and religious ceremonies.

The second section begins with chapter 25 and goes to the end of the book, with the exception of chapters 32 through 34. This large portion of Exodus concerns the Tabernacle, the place where the holy God would manifest His mercy and grace to a sinful people through an elaborate system of sacrifices.

We have already mentioned in these studies that Exodus is a book of contrasts. We have seen how Moses, in a superb act of faith, identified himself with his people, only to fall immediately into an act of human folly. We have seen, on several occasions, how Israel experienced great victory, only to fall prey to bitter murmurings and threaten rebellion.

But none of these contrasts equals the one which forms our present chapter. In fact, these events are unbelievable except when considered in the light of the deep depravity of human nature and the power of evil.

Israel had just lived through one of the most dramatic and awesome experiences ever accorded a nation. The people had been exposed to the power and glory of God manifested in the terrifying physical phenomena proceeding from Mount Sinai. They had heard God's voice. They had entered into a solemn covenant with Him and promised Him their obedience.

Then, some 40 days later, while the glory of God was still present on the mountain height, they sank to the depths of degradation, aided by Aaron himself.

Before God gave Moses the Law on the mountain, He had exacted a covenant of obedience from the people. They had said, "All that the Lord hath spoken we will do." The Lord had descended upon the mountain and Moses had entered into His presence, where he had received the words of the Law. Now that the Law was given, God exacted a ratification of this covenant in a solemn ceremony at the foot of the mount.

I. The Ratification of the Covenant (Exod. 24)

The Lord called Moses, along with Aaron, his two sons, and seventy of the elders to separate themselves from the people by climbing to a higher level of the mountain. Only Moses, however, was allowed to enter into the presence of God in the cloud.

1. The promise of obedience (vv. 3, 7). Moses recited, possibly in resume, the words of the Law to the people, and they answered as with one voice, "All the words which the Lord hath said will we do."

He then wrote in a book in detail all the words that God had given him. After having built an altar and offered sacrifices upon it, he read these words to the people, and they again agreed to them, saying, "All that the Lord hath said we will do, and be obedient."

2. The blood of the covenant (vv. 4-6, 8). Following the instructions given at the close of chapter 20, Moses built an altar. He surrounded it with 12 pillars representing the tribes. Young men (the priesthood was not yet formalized) offered sacrifices upon this altar, and the blood was divided. Half of it was sprinkled upon the altar, representing God's part of the covenant, and the other part upon the people, as Moses said, "Behold, the blood of the covenant."

This was a solemn and momentous occasion, far more than a mere verbal assent, binding people and leaders to the covenant.

3. The vision of God (vv. 9-11). The covenant having been ratified, God then bade Moses, Aaron and his sons, and the elders to mount even higher, and there He revealed himself in His glory. This was not, of course, a visible representation of God, but the glory they saw was compared to a paved work of sapphire having the brilliance of the heavens.

4. Moses in the mountain (vv. 12-18). Jehovah then separated Moses from the others, calling him higher into the mount of God. Joshua accompanied him, at least part way. Formal instructions were given to Aaron and Hur to deal with any matters that would arise during the absence of Moses. For six days Moses waited outside the cloud of glory that covered the mountain. Then, on the seventh day he entered the cloud, disappearing from the sight of the Israelites. For forty days and nights he was there, neither eating nor drinking (Deut. 9:9). God gave him the sacred tablets of stone upon which were written by the divine finger the words of the Law. But there was more: it was at this time that God revealed to Moses His grace by showing Him the pattern of the Tabernacle, by which sinful man would have access to a holy God.

Moses had known the 40 years of the desert; now he was experiencing 40 days of ecstasy in the presence of God.

II. The Folly of the Israelites (Exod. 32)

It is difficult to know just how to read this chapter. One can attempt to rationalize the conduct of the children of Israel by remembering that just short months previously they had been slaves in idolatrous Egypt and had doubtless participated in much of the debauchery of that land. Yet in the context of what had just happened, their conduct seems fantastically unbelievable. While the presence of Jehovah was still visible on the mountain heights, they sank to an act of idolatry whose shame is unparalleled in human history.

1. The construction of the golden calf (vv. 1-6). During the first several days of Moses' sojourn on the mountain the people's hearts burned with the intensity of what they had seen and heard. Yet life had to go on, and the mundane affairs of existence gradually reassumed their importance.

As the days progressed, excitement turned to indifference, but indifference gradually turned to alarm when Moses failed to return. Forty days is an eternity when someone is expected to arrive momentarily. Little did they realize that there was more that God wanted them to know. Certainly Moses had perished on the mountainside! Who would lead them now? Where was the God who had spoken to them from the fire? They needed gods like all the other nations, or they would perish in the desert.

These and many other thoughts filled their hearts as fear gradually replaced faith. It seems evident in these verses that Aaron was lax in his leadership, for he who had seen God's glory should have been able to lead the people in their worship of God, even during Moses' absence. But whatever may have happened, the mob finally controlled, and the people massed themselves before Aaron demanding that he make them gods that would go before them. "As for this Moses, we know not what is become of him."

Aaron's compliance is inexplicable. Perhaps the people threatened him, but even so, courage and steadfastness on his part could have turned the tide. Perhaps his action was a form of compromise, he thinking that they could worship the true Jehovah under the guise of a visible representation. He doubtless did not foresee the debauchery that would follow. Calling for their gold ornaments, he fashioned the image of a calf, a representation of the gods they had seen in Egypt. Did he think that the people would turn away from it in disgust? But the multitude cried, "These be thy gods, O Israel, which brought thee up out of the land of Egypt." At this, Aaron made an altar and proclaimed a feast to Jehovah the following day, doubtless hoping still to save the situation. But they were just using him. The mob had control. Aaron's inferiority to his younger brother is revealed with graphic shame.

It is ironic to note that the final day of Moses' absence

was the day that Aaron gave in to the people's folly. Had he but resisted another 24 hours, Moses would have returned, and he could have met him with honor and dignity. What a lesson for those who are struggling against evil in their lives!

Though it is useless to try to explain the conduct of the Israelites on this day of debauchery, there are several observations we should make.

First, one cannot judge the true character of people simply on the basis of emotional commitments. The Israelites had solemnly pledged obedience to God both before and after the giving of the Law, but in both cases the atmosphere was charged with emotion. When the emotion passed, the commitment was forgotten.

To say this does not imply that we should try to bypass emotional situations. We should not. God used them, and so can we. Emotion is what brings the richness to our spiritual life. However, an emotionally triggered decision does not always indicate a true commitment.

There is quite a lot of high-speed, high-pressure soul-winning in Christian circles today. In many cases the result is true conversion; in many other cases it is nothing but a psychologically induced "yes" response which will last no longer than the time spent to exact it. Genuine repentance from a lifetime of sin takes more than a smile and a slap on the back, and the quality of the repentance usually indicates the quality of the conversion. We cannot engineer the Holy Spirit into our patterns of dealing with people. He wants to use us, not the contrary.

Second, this story should tell us that even the most dramatic manifestations can become commonplace. When the mountain first smoked with the fire of God's presence, the people trembled. But after the 40 days of waiting, this same smoking mountain was ignored in an orgy of idolatry.

Time heals, but it also dulls. If we expect to live our Christian lives from the excitement of one experience to another, without knowing the satisfaction of an ever-deepening daily communion with the Lord, we shall find that when legitimate experiences fail to stimulate, we shall begin to find our thrills in those that are forbidden.

Third, this story teaches us that human reasoning must never be substituted for divine revelation. God had explicitly commanded His people, first, never to worship any other gods, and second, never to worship Him under the form of images. Aaron was well aware of this, but nevertheless, he substituted his own reasoning for God's revelation. Perhaps he thought the Israelites were too fresh out of Egypt for such an abrupt command. Perhaps, on the contrary, he felt that the sight of an idol would be so repulsive to them that they would see their folly. Whatever he reasoned, his mistake was to follow his reasoning instead of God's Word.

We can reason about revelation in order better to understand what God meant when He spoke. This is what we do when we study the Scriptures. But we can never substitute our reason for revelation. This is rationalism. Yet traces of rationalism are always present in every church, and in every denomination, when the non-biblical aspects of our Christianity are given the same value as those based on the Scriptures, or when we ignore the spirit of the Scriptures by making the words say something they were never meant to say.

Fourth, we learn from Aaron that compromise is no substitute for courage. Perhaps he reasoned that he could meet them halfway—allowing them to have an idol just as long as they used it to worship Jehovah. He could not see that the law is a unity, and that when one commandment is ignored the others will also be forgotten. By the time their riotous festivities were over, the Children of Israel had made a shambles of all the commandments, just because Aaron had been willing to compromise on one point.

Finally, this story teaches us that though the Law provides the standard for righteousness, it can never provide the power. The Israelites had woefully disobeyed their Creator, but how many times have we not done the same, though in less dramatic circumstances? "Who shall deliver me from the body of this death?" cries Paul. There is only one answer: Christ Jesus. "What the law could not do, in that it was weak through the flesh, God sending his own Son in the likeness of sinful flesh, and for sin, condemned sin in the flesh; that the righteousness of the law might be fulfilled in us, who walk not after the flesh, but after the Spirit" (Rom. 8:3-4).

2. **The intercession of Moses (vv. 7-14).** Jehovah announces to Moses the sin of the people, calling them "thy people," and saying that He will destroy them and make of Moses a great nation.

Immediately this great man of God intercedes on their behalf. First, he reminds God that the Israelites are His people, not Moses' for it was He, and not Moses, who was responsible for bringing them out of the land of Egypt.

Second, he reminds God of the consequences that their destruction would bring. The news would get back to Egypt, and the name of this One who had done such mighty works would be dishonored.

Third, he brings before God the covenant that He made with Abraham, with Isaac, and with Jacob—the promise to multiply their posterity and bring them into the land of promise.

Heeding the intercession of His servant, God repents: He changes His attitude toward the sinning people. There is profound mystery in this statement, "God repented," but also profound comfort. Though God is unchanging in His purposes, and though God lives in eternity, He nevertheless heeds the prayers of His servants in His temporal dealings with man.

3. **Moses' wrath (vv. 19-24).** Now it is Moses' turn to manifest his wrath. When on the mountain, in the rapture of fellowship with Him who is all purity, he could not fathom the immensity of Israel's sin. But now he descends from the

mountain and meets Joshua on a lower level. They approach the plateau where the Israelites are camped, and Joshua says he hears the noise of war. Coming nearer, Moses exclaims that it is the noise of singing. They quicken their pace.

Then, turning the final bend of the rocky trail, they break upon the horrible scene spread out before them. Moses cannot contain himself, and in a great outburst of passion he casts the divinely inscribed tables of the Law onto the rocks below. He storms into the midst of the debauchery, ignoring the cowering Aaron, burns the idol, and grinds its remains into powder, forcing the people to drink the water into which this powder has been sprinkled.

Then, he turns to his brother, "What did this people unto thee, that thou hast brought so great a sin upon them?" Moses, fresh from the presence of God, is stunned into disbelief at the scene he has just witnessed from the people who so solemnly pledged themselves to obedience. Aaron attempts to excuse himself, implying that the golden calf was an act of providence—that it just happened to come out this way. His confession is as cowardly as was his yielding to the Israelite mob.

We are not told all that happened on this encounter of the two brothers, but we are told in another passage that had not Moses interceded for Aaron, he would have been slain (Deut. 9:20). We can only surmise that this weak brother was snatched back to his senses, and seeing the enormity of his deed, humbled himself before Jehovah. Ever after, entering the Tabernacle in the garments of the high priest, he would be conscious of his unworthiness.

4. The judgment of the rebellious (vv. 25-29). The sudden appearance of Moses had instantly sobered the vast majority of the sinning people. Further, we do not know how many of the Israelites refused to participate in this idolatry. But looking around. Moses saw that there were still some reveling in their naked debauchery. He stood at the gate and cried out, "Who is on the Lord's side?" All the sons of Levi came to him, and he sent them throughout the camp with drawn swords to slay those who were still unrepentant. Three thousand men died from the sword of the Levites. Moses then called on the people to consecrate themselves.

5. Moses and God (vv. 30-35). Moses resumed his intercession before God. The hour of Israel's deepest depravity had provided the occasion for Moses' finest hour; never was he greater than here and in the two chapters following. One man had stayed the hand of God in judgment. One man had abolished idolatry and had turned the nation back to Jehovah. And now this man promised to return to God to seek to make atonement for their sin.

To attempt an exposition of this prayer is to risk spoiling a thing of fragile beauty. This is not the Moses who shattered the tables of the Law and tore down the idol. His wrath is gone, and it is a broken and disappointed man who now seeks God's face. His sentences are fragmented, and they seem to glisten with the tears that must have coursed down his cheeks. "Yet now, if thou wilt forgive their sin—; and if not, blot me, I pray thee, out of the book which thou hast written." Only Paul prayed a similar prayer, when he said, with great heaviness and continual sorrow, "I could wish that myself were accursed from Christ for my brethren" (Rom. 9:3). Both men had known deep discouragement. But both men knew God as few others have known Him.

We live in a day when we are surrounded by sin as blatant as that of the Israelites, and this in a country which has always prided itself for knowing God's law. The fact that God has not already showered down his plagues is only an indication of His long-suffering.

But how many of us have felt the same wrath that Moses felt when faced with open sin? How many of us have had the courage to speak out boldly, even when alone, against the carnality of man's lawlessness?

And how many of us have felt the same brokenness as this Moses who, returning into the presence of his God, poured out his heart on their behalf, so deeply involved in their sufferings that he was willing to perish with them?

Perhaps it is because few of us have spent much time up on the mountaintop, in the presence of the Lord of glory.

Questions for Discussion

1. Why had God commanded that He not be worshiped under the form of an image?
2. Does the second commandment have anything to do with the possession of pictures representing Jesus?
3. Why does the sin of idolatry usually lead to immorality?
4. Does the debauchery of the Israelites before the golden calf prove that they were not sincere when they pledged themselves to obedience?
5. How can we reconcile the immutability of God with the fact that he "repented" as a result of Moses' prayer?
6. Is it humanly possible to desire to be cursed for the sake of our brethren?

13

Jehovah of Glory

Exodus 33–34

I. The Repentance of Israel (Exod. 33:1-11)
   1. The command to depart (vv. 1-3)
   2. The repentance of the people (vv. 4-6)
   3. Israel's reconciliation with Jehovah (vv. 7-11)

II. The Prayer of Moses (Exod. 33:12-23)
   1. The request for God's presence (vv. 13-17)
   2. The request for God's glory (vv. 18-23)

III. The Glory of the Lord (Exod. 34)
   1. Jehovah's glory revealed (vv. 5-9)
   2. The glory reflected (vv. 29-35)

Man's rebellion against God is one of the great mysteries of the universe. The God who lives in eternity knew before the creation that His subjects would revolt against His lordship; yet He created them anyway. The Jehovah who solemnly ratified the covenant with the Children of Israel knew that in some 40 days they would be debasing themselves before an idol; yet He accepted them at their word.

Though God does not cause sin, He nevertheless permits it. The love He wants from His creatures is not a forced love; it must spring from the hearts of men who are free. Further, and here the mystery deepens, only those who have known sin can really know the God of love.

The Prodigal Son thought that he knew his father before he left home. And he did know him, in a certain manner. But it was only when he returned weeping into his father's arms that he began to know him fully.

Spiritual greatness has many facets, and we have examined several of them in these lessons. In its essence, however, spiritual greatness means knowing God, and knowing Him fully. Israel's sin was a terrible act of folly, but through it the people learned to know God as they had not known Him before. And because of their sin, Moses was given the privilege of beholding the glory of Jehovah.

The golden calf had been destroyed, the altar was torn down, and the Levites had gone through the camp with drawn sword executing God's judgment. At least one night had passed since the idolatrous revelry of the Jews, and now, when we read the end of chapter 32 and the beginning of chapter 33, we can sense the heaviness of the atmosphere that pervaded the camp of God's people, mute with guilt and shame.

Yet it is from this soil of heaviness that springs this choice blossom of the Book of Exodus. These chapters are the spiritual high point of the book; it is here that God reveals himself in one of the richest passages of the Pentateuch.

I. The Repentance of Israel (Exod. 33:1-11)

1. The command to depart (vv. 1-3). The Lord commands

Moses to gather together the people and depart for the land which He promised to Abraham, Isaac, and Jacob, the land flowing with milk and honey. The words of this command are nearly identical to previous promises that Jehovah had given to the people.

But there is one difference—a difference which changes the whole character of the command. Whereas previously we read, "The Lord shall bring thee into the land," here God says, "I will send an angel before thee." Further, He says, "I will not go up in the midst of thee, for thou art a stiff-necked people, lest I consume thee in the way."

God would give them the land, but He would not go with them. Actually, this is what many people want in their religion; blessings but not God. Yet Israel readily recognized the impossibility of this proposal. They had but one claim to greatness—the fact that Jehovah was with them. Without His presence they were nothing, and their nation would disintegrate.

2. The repentance of the people (vv. 4-6). When Moses related this to the people, they mourned. They immediately sensed the enormity of their sin and the hopelessness of their situation. God said, "Ye are a stiff-necked people; I will come up into the midst of thee in a moment and consume thee." Yet even in these stern words there is a hint of mercy, for God then commanded them to take off their ornaments. As an outward sign of their repentance they stripped themselves of all the trappings of gaiety.

3. Israel's reconciliation with Jehovah (vv. 7-11). Moses took the tabernacle and pitched it outside the camp. This is not, of course, the Tabernacle which God had just commanded him to construct. It was a tent that served in some way as a meeting place between God and man, perhaps prefiguring the true Tabernacle to be made after the heavenly pattern.

Here Moses awaited the repentant people. They came, and as they came, Moses would enter the tabernacle to intercede for them with Jehovah. Each time he entered, the cloudy pillar descended, signifying God's presence. The people showed their reverence by standing at the door of their tents worshiping God. The Lord talked with Moses as with a friend, face to face.

These verses are rich in imagery. The tent was taken outside the camp of the Israelites, for the entire congregation had polluted itself, and God could be no longer in its midst. Only Moses and Joshua were free from the taint of the golden calf, and thus it was these two who had the privilege of entering the tabernacle. But not only did Moses have the privilege of communing with God; he also was able to stand between God and man to bring reconciliation to those who had gone astray.

II. The Prayer of Moses (Exod. 33:12-23)

After Moses had accomplished his priestly function of bringing reconciliation to the people, he reasoned with God concerning the future. His mind was in a state of anxious inquiry, and he came before the Lord to have all his pressing perplexities solved.

Several doubts tormented this man of God as a result of the broken covenant and Jehovah's stern words. He felt even more intensely the weight of this rebellious people he was to lead, and wanted God to explain what He meant when He said an angel would go before them. "See, thou sayest unto me, bring up this people, and thou hast not let me know whom thou wilt send with me."

Moses' prayer contained two main requests.

1. The request for God's presence (vv. 13-17). "Shew me now thy way, that I may know thee, that I may find grace in thy sight; and consider that this nation is thy people."

In this same place, months previously, Jehovah had appeared from the burning bush to a broken Moses and commanded him to deliver the Children of Israel from their Egyptian bondage. When Moses had protested his unworthiness, Jehovah had replied, "Certainly I will be with thee."

Now, in spite of all the manifestations of God's power and presence, Israel had sunk to the depths of spiritual degradation. So great was their sin that God's presence would destroy them; these were the words Moses had heard the day before.

But if Israel had sinned greatly, so had they repented. Would this change God's attitude toward them? questioned Moses. Jehovah had revealed His mercy in not utterly annihilating His sinful people; now Moses pleaded for His grace, reminding the Lord that "this nation is thy people." Only His presence, not that of an angel, could guarantee their entrance into the land of promise.

The response of the Lord is an Old Testament gem: "My presence will go with you, and I will give you rest."

Rest comes not in changing circumstances, but in an unchanging God. With these words God restored inner peace to His troubled servant.

Moses continued: "If thy presence go not with me, carry us not up hence." It was folly to consider going on without Him. His grace could be revealed only in one way—by His presence; only this would separate them from the other peoples of the earth and assure their holiness.

"I will do this thing also that thou hast spoken," answers the Lord, "for thou hast found grace in my sight, and I know thee by name."

In these crisis days we must increasingly realize—not just from the lips but from the heart—that the church's only claim to success is the presence of God. From a material standpoint the church has never been greater. She is well organized and rich. But it is only as she manifests the glory of God that she has meaning in this world.

When Jesus announced His departure, the disciples were greatly saddened. Yet Jesus told them it was better for Him to leave so that the Comforter would come. Jesus was with them, and in this way Jesus' presence would accompany His scattered disciples as they carried His Word to the ends of the earth.

One of those who knew this presence in an intimate way was Paul. When speaking of the troubles that beset him on every side, he said, "Though our outward man perish, yet the inward man is renewed day by day" (2 Cor. 4:16). Few have known the pressures that Paul faced, but for him, stability did not depend on outward circumstances. If he was able to know inner renewal, it was because he knew Christ intimately. "Christ is my life," said he, and the intense desire of his heart was to know Him better.

2. The request for God's glory (vv. 18-23). Moses dared make one more request. God had promised to go with him, but to banish all doubts, Moses asked to see His glory.

Moses had already known God in a way few men have known Him. Just 40 days previously, with the elders of Israel, he had seen the glory of God revealed on the mountain. But much had happened since; the former vision was at a time of national exultation. Since, the nation had been brought to its knees. God had promised mercy and grace, but Moses begged for a new vision of God to give him assurance under these new and sobering circumstances.

The Lord complied with Moses' request. And in doing so, He revealed His character in a new way. "I will be gracious to whom I will be gracious, and will shew mercy on whom I will shew mercy." Israel had sinned as a nation, and deserved national chastisement. But God's mercy and grace, even in national disgrace, would continue to be revealed to individuals. Just as He knew Moses by name, so did He know individually the members of this great nation, and national sin would not cause faithful individuals to forfeit their eternal blessings.

No man could see the face of Jehovah: His face represented the full outshining of His glory; no one in the flesh could bear this and live. Therefore the Lord set Moses in a cleft of the rock and covered his eyes when He passed by, allowing him to see only the after glory—the luminous reflection of what He was.

Only a few men have seen God's glory as did Moses. Some, called to exceptional missions, have had exceptional visions of His majesty, such as the disciples who saw Jesus transfigured on the mountain. John, writing of this experience, says, "We beheld his glory" (John 1:14).

But though few have had these spectacular experiences, all men who would know spiritual greatness must know God's glory. Nothing can replace this—talents, personality, or education—for those who are called to a spiritual mission. And to know God's glory, we must take the time and arrange the circumstances of our lives to permit us to behold it.

Unfortunately, when most people think of God, they do not think of glory. Worship for many Christians is unappealing; for some it is even distasteful. Christians willingly spend hours beholding TV; many would be startled if someone ever asked them how much time they spend beholding His glory. Moses spent 40 days in rapture before God, and this experience was repeated. For the average Christian, 40 minutes spent in private worship would seem like an eternity. Yet what else is eternity than this? For heaven means beholding the glory of God in its fulness.

Somehow we have succeeded in creating the impression that worship is just a duty—just as we have with reading the Bible, praying, and witnessing. But how absurd can we be? If we are created in the image of a personal God, who is wise and great enough to make the universe with all its wonders and mysteries, and loving enough to send His Son to die on the cross in a spectacular victory over evil, what should be more thrilling than worship? I shall never forget the sheer pleasure of finally realizing, after trying faithfully to endure my daily religious duties for several years so that I could get quickly on to more attractive things, that I had seen it all backwards. Worship is not primarily duty; it is privilege and joy, and the highest joy known to man and that which gives him his deepest sense of fulfillment and reality.

Let us get all the training we can get for God's service. Let us organize our churches as well as we can. But let us never forget all this becomes empty if we fail to behold His glory.

III. The Glory of the Lord (Exod. 34)

In this chapter Moses once again spent 40 days and nights in the presence of Jehovah. But even though the Lord had manifested His mercy and grace to His sinning people, His character remained unchanged, and thus it was necessary for Him to renew two things with His people: the Law and the covenant.

Before going up into the mountain, Moses was therefore commanded to hew out new tables on which God would again inscribe the Law. God had hewed out the first ones, but Moses had shattered them; now Moses must hew out new tables, though God would write upon them.

Then, after being in the mountain and once again pleading for the Lord's presence in the midst of the people, Moses received a renewal of the covenant (vv. 10-28). Jehovah would do wonders for His people if they would keep themselves pure from unholy alliances with the pagan nations. The Lord is a jealous God; the people must worship no other gods and make no graven images. They must keep the feasts and sabbaths, and redeem the firstborn of their numbers. They must avoid the pagan practices of the other nations, and if they did this, God would protect them in the land of promise.

1. Jehovah's glory revealed (vv. 5-9). Alone in the mountain Moses had communion with the Jehovah of glory. This glory, however, was not simply an undefined brightness; it was represented by His name. "The Lord descended in the cloud, and stood with him there and proclaimed the name of the Lord." Here God revealed the glory of His name in much the same way that the glory of a ray of light is revealed as it passes through a prism. This rich spectrum divides into seven characteristics of God's nature, three pairs referring to His mercy and a single one referring to His justice.

Jehovah is merciful and gracious. God revealed His will to

His nation, but she constantly demonstrated her inability to abide by it. Israel, by her murmurings and idolatry, merited God's destruction. Speaking in His holiness, God had said He would consume her; but His character is not limited to holiness—He is also a God of mercy, and in mercy He withheld the judgment that this sinning nation merited.

Through His mercy God withholds the punishment we deserve, through His grace He accords the blessing we do not deserve. Because of His mercy, God did not destroy the sinning people; because of His grace, God promised to continue to accompany them by His own presence.

Jehovah is long-suffering and abundant in goodness and truth. In this statement He reveals His mercy and grace in two new dimensions. First, He tells us that He is long-suffering. This means that His mercy and grace are continual attributes. When one reads the accounts of the Children of Israel in the wilderness, he is amazed to see how patient God was with His rebellious people. But is He not also patient with us? He does not promise to forgive us just one time, but each time we confess our sins. Were it not for His attitude of long-suffering toward us, we could never hope to see Him, for each new sin would bring judgment.

Second, His mercy and truth are abundant. Mercy and truth must go together; this is why complete honesty is necessary when we approach God. To try to deceive Him is to deceive ourselves; because God is truth, we must be true with Him. The word "abundant" reveals a second dimension to His mercy. Mercy is long-suffering in the sense that it is continually poured out; it is abundant in the sense that it is great enough for even the greatest disobedience. Some feel that their sins are too great to be forgiven. God's mercy is yet greater.

Keeping mercy for thousands, forgiving iniquity and transgression and sin. In this third pair of God's attributes His mercy is revealed in still two more dimensions. First, it is not limited to one or two individuals; it is for thousands. The supply never runs out. To be sure, God's goodness is limited by man's unwillingness to receive it, but from the divine standpoint God is ready to pour out mercy upon all who come to Him, not just a few favored individuals.

Second, it is not limited to any particular kind of sin. God forgives sins that are great in the sense of quantity; He also forgives sins that are great in the sense of quality. Three words are used here to describe wrongdoing, and these three words cover every possible kind of sin.

Jehovah will by no means clear the guilty. The last of these seven characteristics seems a contradiction of the others. However, this is not a contradiction; God's mercy can only be manifested through His justice. Forgiveness is not an empty thing; sin cannot go unpunished, as was seen in the continual sacrifice of the animals and later in the supreme sacrifice of God himself at the cross. Blood atonement is distasteful only to those who do not know the justice of God. Further, God's mercy, though available to the thousands, is experienced only by those who are willing to receive it in God's way. And so terrible is sin that even when its eternal consequences are eradicated, its temporal consequences are felt by children and children's children. This the Israelites would know during the 40 years of wandering.

Thus does God reveal His glory. When we seek to worship the God of glory, let us remember that worship is not simply an emotional feeling toward an impersonal force. It is an intelligent act of praise of one person for another. We should worship, said Jesus, in spirit (this doubtless has reference to the eternal part of man's personality, mainly his mind and will) and in truth (this means to worship God as He really is, revealed in His Word, and not as something empty and undefined).

2. The glory reflected (vv. 29-35). When Moses returned from the mountain experience with Jehovah, his face shone in a reflection of the glory he had experienced. He was not aware of his changed appearance until the people retreated from him in fear. To enable him to talk to the people and deliver to them all the Lord had commanded him on the mount, a veil was put over his face. Whenever he went before the people, the veil was put on; then, when he would go into the presence of God, he would remove it.

Thus it was that Moses reached the peak of his spiritual greatness in the eyes of his people. Seeing him with the glory shining from his face, who could doubt that God had met with him and had once again proved His mercy and grace? What a contrast from the first descent from the mountain after the first 40 days, when the people were in idolatrous revelry and the tables of the Law were shattered to pieces.

Because Moses had been with God, he reflected His glory. Our spiritual greatness reaches its peak when we, too, reflect His glory, not our own. Paul, in 2 Corinthians 3, talks of the old covenant and of the glory that shone on Moses' face, saying that the glory of the new is far greater. Then, in a remarkable ending to this chapter, he exclaims, "We all, with open face, beholding as in a glass the glory of the Lord, are changed into the same image, from glory to glory, even as by the Spirit of the Lord" (2 Cor. 3:18).

We are God's epistle to men—written not on tables of stone, but on the tables of the heart—to be read of all men. We are to reflect the glory of God, just as Moses reflected it when he descended from the mountaintop. It is not an undefined glory that we are to reflect; God is real, and the realities of His personality can be reflected in ours. If God is merciful and gracious, so must we be if men would see Him. If God is long-suffering and abundant in goodness and truth, so can we be. If God's mercy extends to all kinds of people and all kinds of sin, so can ours. If God's mercy manifests itself in justice, so must we by our actions present to men the justice of God.

"Let your light so shine before men that they may see your good works, and glorify your Father which is in heaven" (Matt. 5:16).

Questions for Discussion

1. If it is through our disobedience that we know God better, should we be thankful for our disobedience?
2. How can we explain the fact that He first says He will not go with them, then promises His presence? Relate this to prayer.
3. Is it possible for us to know God's grace without knowing His presence?
4. How, in a practical way in twentieth-century America, can we meaningfully behold the glory of God?
5. What are ways to make worship more natural and meaningful?
6. Does manifesting the glory of the Lord mean having a different physical appearance?
7. What does it mean to glorify God?

ADDITIONAL STUDY GUIDES IN THIS SERIES . .

GENESIS, John P. Burke, $3.95.
EXODUS, Tom Julien, $3.95.
DEUTERONOMY, Bernard N. Schneider, $3.95.
JOSHUA, JUDGES & RUTH, John J. Davis, $3.95.
1 & 2 SAMUEL & 1 KINGS 1-11, John J. Davis, $3.95.
KINGS & CHRONICLES, John C. Whitcomb, $3.95.
PROVERBS, Charles W. Turner, $3.95.
MATTHEW, Harold H. Etling, $3.95.
GOSPEL OF JOHN, Homer A. Kent, Jr., $3.95.
ACTS, Homer A. Kent, Jr., $3.95.
ROMANS, Herman A. Hoyt, $3.95.
1 CORINTHIANS, James L. Boyer, $3.95.
GALATIANS, Homer A. Kent, Jr., $3.95.
EPHESIANS, Tom Julien, $3.95.
PHILIPPIANS, David L. Hocking, $3.95.
1 & 2 TIMOTHY, Dean Fetterhoff, $3.95.
HEBREWS, Herman A. Hoyt, $3.95.
JAMES, Roy R. Roberts, $3.95.
1, 2, 3 JOHN, Raymond E. Gingrich, $3.95.
REVELATION, Herman A. Hoyt, $3.95.
THE WORLD OF UNSEEN SPIRITS, Bernard N. Schneider, $3.95.
THE HOLY SPIRIT AND YOU, Bernard N. Schneider, $3.95.
PROPHECY, THINGS TO COME, James L. Boyer, $3.95.
PULPIT WORDS TRANSLATED FOR PEW PEOPLE,
  Charles W. Turner, $3.95.
SWEETER THAN HONEY, Jesse B. Deloe *(A guide to effective Bible study and the background of how we got our Bible),* $3.95.
THE FAMILY FIRST, Kenneth O. Gangel, $2.50.

Obtain from your local Christian bookstore or by mail from BMH Books, P.O. Box 544, Winona Lake, Ind. 46590. (Include a check with your order and BMH Books pays postage.)